John Towler

The Negative and Print

The Photographer's Guide in the Gallery and in the Field

John Towler

The Negative and Print
The Photographer's Guide in the Gallery and in the Field

ISBN/EAN: 9783337805111

Printed in Europe, USA, Canada, Australia, Japan

Cover: Foto ©Thomas Meinert / pixelio.de

More available books at **www.hansebooks.com**

THE

NEGATIVE AND THE PRINT;

OR,

THE PHOTOGRAPHER'S GUIDE,

IN THE

GALLERY AND IN THE FIELD,

BEING A

TEXT-BOOK FOR THE OPERATOR AND AMATEUR,

Containing Brief and Concise Instructions for the Preparation of the
Different Kinds of Photographs now in Vogue.

SUCH AS THE

*Ordinary Negative for Contact Printing, the Solar Negative, and
the Negative for the Copying Camera; Printing on Albumen
Paper; Vignette Printing; Printing Positives on Opal or Plain
Glass; the Ambrotype, Ferrotype, Melainotype, etc.; Stereo-
graphic Printing; the Dry Process; the Construction of the
Glass-House; the Camera and the Lens; and the Treatment of
the Gold and Silver Residues.*

BY

JOHN TOWLER, M. D.,

PROFESSOR OF CHEMISTRY, NATURAL PHILOSOPHY, AND MATHE-
MATICS IN HOBART COLLEGE; AUTHOR OF "THE SILVER
SUNBEAM," "THE PORCELAIN PICTURE," AND
EDITOR OF "HUMPHREY'S JOURNAL
OF PHOTOGRAPHY," ETC.

NEW YORK:
JOSEPH H. LADD, PUBLISHER, No. 600 BROADWAY.
1866.
—————
HUMPHREY'S JOURNAL PRINT.

CONTENTS.

PHOTOGRAPHER'S GUIDE.

CHAPTER I.

PREPARATION OF THE GLASS PLATES FOR THE RECEPTION OF THE COLLODION FILM.

IT is almost unnecessary to assert, that the finest and clearest plate glass is the best adapted for photographic purposes, the only objection is the expense. If the practical photographer lays in a stock of glass in large plates, it becomes necessary to construct a table for the special purpose of cutting up the large plates of glass into the sizes required. Any ordinary table about four feet long and three feet wide will be suitable for this purpose. Let the upper surface be planed perfectly level and smooth, and afterwards covered with green baize. Along two sides and one end a slip of hard wood is fixed upon the baize; this slip is one inch wide and about one-sixteenth of an inch in thickness; that is, slightly thinner than any glass plate that may be required to be cut. These slips are graduated into inches and fractional parts of an inch along the two sides, beginning at the angle in each case and proceeding to the left. A flat rule is next required, about three feet and a half in length, two inches wide, and half an inch thick; it must be of

1

hard wood, and perfectly straight along the edges. Finally, a glazier's diamond is the next requisite. The operator must go to a glazier, if he does not know how to use the diamond. He will learn more in five minutes in this respect than we could impart to him by a lengthy description. The cut of a diamond on glass, when correctly made, is like the cut of a sharp knife when the edge of the blade is drawn along the surface of a piece of wood; it is a wedge-like incision totally distinct from a scratch. When the cut is made, the next thing is to separate the two parts; this is effected by partly bending and partly pulling the two pieces assunder, beginning at one side and proceeding gradually, though quickly onwards, to the other side. Naturally the incision made by the diamond must be complete to the edge, otherwise the fracture will not easily commence; and if the incision does not reach the opposite side, the fracture may deviate from a straight line at the part where the diamond cut is defective.

The operator has to find out in what position his diamond makes a cut, and not a scratch, and then he can ever afterwards fix it in this position.

The glass cutting operation is performed on and near the right end of the table; in consequence of this, the left end is comparatively free and may be set aside to receive the vice, etc., for polishing the plates with buckskin; whilst the drawer on the side will be a suitable receptacle for the diamond, files, buffers, buckskin, silk and linen cloths, and whatever else may be needed in this department. A certain portion of the drawer may be divided off into compartments for the reception of the different sized plates used, as, for instance, for card-pictures, cabinet-pictures, etc.

The plates being now in readiness for the next step, the sharp edges are all abraded by means of a file kept for this purpose. Whilst performing this work, the back of the operator is turned towards the table, in order that the fine particles of abraded glass may fall upon the floor and not upon the green baize on the table.

The next operation is to ascertain by actual trial that each abraded plate will fit in the shield of the plateholder; for it is a very vexatious trouble to find, after the plate has been covered, with collodion and sensitized, that it is too large for the holder. After each trial, and when found correct in size, the plate is put away in its special receptacle until required.

Whether the plates have been used before, or not, we recommend that they be placed in a bath of nitric acid and water of the following strength:

Nitric acid - - - - - 2 ounces.
Water - - - - - 2 pints.

They may remain in this bath for six or eight hours; by this steeping the old films of varnish and collodion are easily separated, whilst with fresh plates the surfaces become thoroughly cleaned from adhering and extraneous substances. Instead of the preceding bath the following is also highly to be recommended:

CAREY LEA'S BATH.

Sulphuric acid - - - - 2 ounces.
Bichromate of potash - - - 2 "
Water - - - - - 2 pints.

The result is about the same whichever bath is used.

The adhering films of varnish, collodion, and albumen are likewise easily removed by immersing the plates in cold water and raising the latter to the boiling temperature. This is the least expensive method but not always the most convenient.

After the plates have thus received their first cleaning, or the first preparation preparatory to washing, each one is taken and placed beneath the tap and submitted to a thorough washing with a clean sponge or the fingers; the stream of water is finally allowed to play upon either side in succession, and then the plate is ready to receive a coating of albumen upon one side.

The best and easiest mode of preparing the albumen solution in stock is probably the one lately published by Mr. Ackland in his modified Fothergill process. The author says it may be preserved in good condition for years *if kept closely corked*.

" Separate the yolks from the whites of any number of eggs, and to every eight ounces of albumen thus obtained add twenty drops of glacial acetic acid previously diluted with one ounce of water; stir these together with a glass rod until intimately mixed, which occupies about one minute; then, after resting one hour, strain through coarse muslin, and to the strained liquid add half a drachm of the strongest liquor ammoniæ; then preserve in carefully corked bottles."

An ounce of this solution diluted with five ounces of water forms a liquid which is suitable for the substratum on glass surfaces. Pour a sufficient quantity of this solution upon the bottom of a clean flat porcelain dish so as just to cover two slips of glass placed along each end of the dish when lying flat, and remove all bubbles with a small piece of paper.

Now take the plate of glass, which has just been thoroughly washed, and resting one end upon the slip of glass at the bottom of the dish, let the plate gradually fall upon the surface of the albumen until the other end rests upon the second slip of glass. A silver hook will be found very convenient for lowering and raising the plate. Now raise the end, lift the plate up and examine its surface. The difficulty in this operation consists in getting a clean surface free from all sort of particles. It frequently happens that such particles are met with on the first film or two. In this case, take the plate to the tap and wash off the albumen thoroughly and begin the operation over again. As soon as the film is quite uniform and without flaw, the plate is allowed to drain for a moment and then put away on the rack to dry in a warm place where there is no current of air to produce dust.

The drying racks referred to are made of strips of corrugated iron; they are indispensable in the laboratory, and can be had of any of our photographic dealers. Several of them will be needed where work is done systematically and with care.

The application of this substratum of albumen saves an immense quantity of labor in cleaning and polishing the glass surfaces by the old method with rotten stone and dilute alcohol; but this saving of labor is but a small part of the advantage gained. With the albumenous substratum, specks, stains, silver reductions on and under the collodion film will seldom or ever occur; and we are not cognizant of a single instance where the collodion film slided off the plate when the albumen was beneath.

The film soon dries and is then indistinguishable from the glass surface as far as appearance goes; but the surface covered with this film can easily be distinguished in case the plates have been misplaced. Glass itself is hygroscopic and retains the breath for some time, whilst, on the contrary, the breath is scarcely retained a moment on the side covered with the albumen.

In large galleries this operation fills up idle time; and in this way a large stock of prepared plates is always on hand and ready at a moment's notice for the next operation. But this brings us to the second chapter.

CHAPTER II.

COLLODION, for photographic purposes, consists of a solution of pyroxyline, or gun-cotton in a mixture of ether and alcohol, to which are added a certain quantity of soluble iodides and bromides, or of either alone according to the purposes for which it is intended. It is not advisable that the operator should manufacture his own gun-cotton ; for he can get it better and cheaper from the dealers, and especially from the chemists who devote their whole and sole attention to its preparation. Nevertheless, we will give our readers the formulas for the preparation of pyroxyline.

There are two distinct methods of making gun-cotton; the former is by means of a mixture of sulphuric acid and nitrate of potash; and the latter of a mixture of sulphuric and of nitric acid. Cotton is immersed in either of these solutions and after remaining a short time it is taken out, washed, and dried. Apparently it has undergone no change ; but by weighing the quantity of cotton before and after the operation we shall find that, after this treatment, the weight has been increased. Furthermore, common cotton is insoluble in ether and alcohol; whilst gun-cotton or pyroxyline is quite soluble in this mixture. Before treatment, too, with the mixed acids cotton will burn, it is true, but it is not an explosive ingredient, as it becomes after impregnation with one of the compounds, oxygen and nitrogen arising from the decomposition of nitric acid.

FIRST METHOD OF PREPARING PYROXYLINE.

Weigh out, in the first place, twelve ounces of pure nitrate of potash, pulverize it and dry it thoroughly before the fire; weigh also twenty-four ounces of sulphuric acid such as is found in commerce; furthermore, weigh out six drachms of clean and well-carded cotton. If the specific gravity of the sulpuric acid is 1.84, one ounce of water is required; if it is as low as 1.836, no water is required; and if it is higher than 1.84, two ounces of water may be measured out and kept in readiness. Separate the cotton into small tufts, and place them also in readiness.

Having next provided a large porcelain evaporating dish, fill it with hot water and let it remain until the vessel is quite warm on the outside. Pour the water out and wipe the dish. Now put in the nitrate of potash, then the water and stir the mixture about for a few seconds. The sulphuric acid is next added and intimately mixed. Finally, the cotton is immersed with rapidity, one tuft at a time, and pushed quite beneath the surface of the mixture and so that every part may come in contact with the acid and salt. Work the cotton about, by means of two glass rods, for about four or five minutes, after the last tuft has been immersed; at the expiration of this time the cotton is taken out and thrown into a large pail of water, where it is well stirred about by means of the glass rods in order to get rid of the major part of the acid.

It is now immersed in a stream of running water, dis-integrated with the fingers, and washed for some time until all acidity has been removed. If a stream of water is not at hand, the washing operation is per-formed in several changes of fresh water; and finally, the pyroxyline, after a thorough wringing, is placed in a vessel of water, made alkaline with a few drops of ammonia. Separate the pyroxyline into small tufts in order that every part may come in contact with the alkali. After remaining in this water for several hours, test the liquid with blue litmus paper; if the latter is not changed in an hour's time, it may be concluded that the acid has been entirely removed.

But now the pyroxyline has to be again washed in several changes of water in order to remove every trace of the alkali. This is a tedious operation, and can easily be dispensed with where there is a regular jet of water in the first instance to remove the acidity.

Wring the pyroxyline, and then separate the matted tufts into thin layers, which may be dried in the sun or on a water bath maintained at a moderate tem-perature.

The weight of the pyroxyline will now be about eight drachms.

SECOND METHOD OF PREPARING PYROXYLINE, BY A MIXTURE OF NITRIC AND OF SULPHURIC ACID.

Make use, as before, of the large, glazed earthen-ware evaporating dish, which is first made warm by floating it on hot water; then pour into it the follow-ing acids:

1*

> Nitric acid, sp. gr. 1.37   -   6 fluid ounces.
> Sulphuric acid, sp. gr. 1.84 - 12   "

Stir the mixture and ascertain the temperature by means of a thermometer. When the thermometer has sunk as low as 150° Fahr., immerse six drachms of well-carded cotton, previously separated into small tufts as before. See that every tuft is thoroughly under the surface; now cover up the dish for ten minutes. At the expiration of this time the cotton is removed by means of the two glass rods; the excess of acid is well pressed out, and then the pyroxyline is plunged into a large bucket of water, and treated in the same way as before described in regard to pyroxyline when prepared with nitrate of potassa, etc.

Ordinary nitric acid has the specific gravity 1.37, but it is well always to test the strength before commencing, because if it be stronger, the relative proportion of the two acids will be different.

Take the following as examples:

No. 1.

> Nitric acid, sp. gr. 1.42   -   9 fluid ounces.
> Sulphuric acid, sp. gr. 1.84 - 9   "
> Cotton   -   -   -   - 6 drachms.

No. 2.

> Nitric acid, sp. gr. 1.40   -   8 fluid ounces.
> Sulphuric acid, sp. gr. 1.84 - 16   "
> Water -   -   -   -   - 1   "
> Cotton   -   -   -   - 6 drachms.

PREPARATION OF PLAIN COLLODION.

The pyroxyline when thoroughly washed and dried

may be preserved in pasteboard boxes for an indefinite time. In order to make collodion of it, it has to be dissolved. It is well to keep a quantity of the dissolved pyroxyline in stock, always ready for mixture with the sensitizing solution. This stock solution is prepared as follows:

Sulphuric ether	-	-	-	2 quarts.
Alcohol	-	-	-	-	1 quart.
Pyroxyline	-	-	-	- 12 drachms.

The pyroxyline soon dissolves in the above mixture, which is well shaken and then put aside in the cellar to settle and ripen. If the pyroxyline is pure and in good condition, there will not be much sediment. Whenever required for use, the proper quantity is decanted from the upper and clear portion at the top by means of a syphon or otherwise. This plain collodion has considerable consistence and may be diluted with alcohol contained in the iodizing solution.

PREPARATION OF BROMO-IODIZED COLLODION.

It is better to keep in stock a sufficient quantity of iodizing solution, by means of which a few ounces of bromo-iodized collodion may be readily prepared. Below will be found three different formulas for these stock solutions:

Formula No. 1.

Landscape Photography.

Iodide of ammonium	-	-	144 grains.
Bromide of cadmium	-	-	120 "
Alcohol	-	-	-	-	12 ounces.

Formula No. 2.

Portrait Photography.

Iodide of cadmium - - -	182 grains.
Bromide of ammonium - -	96 "
Alcohol - - - -	12 "

Formula No. 3.

Landscapes and Portraits.

Iodide of cadmium - - -	108 grains.
Iodide of ammonium - -	108 "
Bromide of ammonium - -	48 "
Alcohol - - - -	12 ounces.

Formula No. 4.

This formula contains no bromide.

Iodide of ammonium - -	144 grains.
Iodide of cadmium - - -	96 "
Chloride of magnesium - -	96 "
Alcohol - - - - -	12 ounces.

These stock solutions have to be kept in a cool dark place, together with the plain collodion; the cellar is a very suitable place. They remain in their present condition unchanged for an indefinite time.

PREPARATION OF IODIZED COLLODION.

Plain collodion - - - -	3 ounces.
Iodizing solution - - - -	1 ounce.

The first and second formulas contain five grains and a half of the mixed bromo-iodides in each ounce of solution; whilst the latter contains six grains to each ounce. The proportions of the salts in the two first

solutions are nearly those of their chemical equiva-
lents.

The quantity of pyroxyline to each ounce of collodion, diluted as indicated by the alcohol in the bromo-
iodizing solution, is six grains to the ounce. More or
less can be added as circumstances require. A more
consistent collodion may be used for very small plates;
whilst a thinner collodion may be found necessary for
large plates; that is, for all sizes above the four-fourth.

If the collodion is not quite clear and free from small
floating particles, it will be found necessary to filter
the solution before it can be used for coating the albumenized plates. Glass filters are manufactured for
this special purpose, which allow the filtration to proceed without exposing the collodion to the atmosphere.
The glass tube with a small aperture at the closed end
is intended to furnish a passage for air from the receiver for a corresponding quantity of collodion that
has filtered through the cotton, that surrounds it at the
bottom, and that drops into the receiver. We prefer
drawing the end of the glass tube into a capillary termination of half or three-quarters of an inch long;
this mode of construction succeeds in preventing the
rising of the collodion up the tube instead of passing
into the receiver, and of thus obstructing the filtration.
These glass filters are very reliable and almost indispensable, if you aim at perfect productions.

In addition to the glass filters, collodion vials are
kept for sale. They are constructed in such a manner
as to prevent bubbles whilst the collodion is being
poured out upon the plate. They are arranged, too, so
as to allow all particles and specks of dry collodion to

accumulate around the neck and not to fall upon the
collodion film. These *comctless* vials, as they are sometimes called, are also very useful and reliable in the
photographic laboratory.

Before the albumenized plate is coated with collodion, ascertain in the first place which side is covered
with albumen, as previously indicated. Secondly, dust
off all particles from this surface by means of a broad
camel's hair pencil, which must stand in a convenient
position for this purpose, reared upon its handle. If
the weather is damp, too, you had better move the
plate a moment or two over a spirit lamp in order to
drive off all moisture; the latter may be seen as it
volatilizes. Then let the plate cool. Hold the plate
by the left front corner between the thumb and first
finger of the left hand, whilst, if the plate be heavy,
the second finger lends assistance in bearing the
weight. The collodion vial is then taken in the right
hand; now pour the collodion upon the plate at the
right hand distant corner, and incline the plate gradually whilst you are pouring, so that the collodion may
flow to the other distant and left hand corner and then
forwards toward the front. As soon as the plate is a
little more than one-half covered, you stop pouring out
any more collodion, and allow that, which has been
already poured upon the plate, to proceed to the front,
by inclining the plate, and so to accumulate near the
right hand anterior corner, where the excess is allowed
to flow back again into the vial. Whilst this excess is
thus dropping off from the corner, oscillate the plate in
the direction of the edge, as if it were poised on this
corner; by doing so ridges on the collodion film in the

direction of the inclination, if the plate were quiescent, may be avoided. As soon as the collodion ceases to drop, or nearly ceases, raise the plate into the horizontal position, and oscillate it now in the direction of the flat surfaces; that is up and down gently; this motion removes all reticulated ridges that might have been formed by the preceding oscillatory motion; and the collodion surface becomes quite smooth.

As soon as the film is no longer soft, when touched with the finger, but yet not perfectly dry, the plate is immersed in the silver bath.

There is a considerable knack in coating a plate successfully with collodion, and this knack, like every mechanical operation of this nature can scarcely be obtained otherwise than by practice. All that we can do is to point out the simplest and clearest method by which the art can be obtained.

To coat very large plates with collodion requires the aid of a pneumatic-holder, which contains at least two suction discs; one of three would still be more expedient. This form of holder has just been patented; it is an excellent aid in such and similar operations, and can be attached in an instant to a plate by simply slapping the discs with a smart quick blow upon the opposite side of the plate to that which it is intended to coat with collodion. A holder with a single disc is sufficiently strong to hold any plate up to the four-fourth size. Another arrangement is found to be very efficacious in coating very large and heavy plates; plates that are much too heavy and too large to be supported by one hand. It is this: a strong walking cane, or, still better, the handle of a broom is fixed perpendicularly in an aperture in the floor; the upper part is rounded off into a semi-spheroidal shape, and a piece of woolen cloth is tied over it. When about to coat the plate, the following is the proceeding: with both hands carry the plate and place it horizontally over the upper end of the broom-stick, so that the center of the plate rests on the woolen cloth; in such a position the plate is easily supported, and, being balanced, it can be oscillated by means of the left hand in any direction whatever. The woolen cloth protects the surface from being scratched, and, at the same time, prevents the plate from sliding off its support. The collodion is poured upon the surface as before directed, and, as soon as the surface is completely covered, the collodion vial is laid aside, and the subsequent manipulations are performed with the two hands acting in combination.

If the collodion film is introduced into the silver bath before it has had time to congeal; that is, has become dry and compact in structure so as not to be disintegrated by an impression from the finger, the film is liable to split up and break off in patches, or wholly, in the subsequent operations of developing, fixing, etc. On the other hand, if the film be too dry, it resists the permeation of the silver solution and does not become, in consequence, so easily and completely sensitized.

CHAPTER III.

THE NITRATE OF SILVER BATH, ITS PREPARATION, TROUBLES, AND RENOVATION.

NITRATE of silver is a salt which is sometimes adulterated; it is an advantage, therefore, to know how to detect this adulteration before the bath is prepared. Buy always the salt in the form of large flat crystalline tables; if the crystals have more the appearance of common salt, it is a pretty certain indication that the salt is not pure.

To make the indication certain, dissolve five grains of the crystals in a drachm of water, and drop into the solution hydrochloric acid as long as a white curdy precipitate is produced; separate the chloride of silver, thus formed, by filtration through paper prepared for the purpose. Into the clear liquid filtrate add another drop of hydrochloric acid; if no curdiness is produced, it is a sign that all the silver has been removed from the solution, which, if the original salt was adulterated, will contain the salt or salts used in the adulteration, together with traces of hydrochloric acid.

Evaporate the filtrate to dryness; if nothing remains on the evaporating dish, it is an evidence that the silver salt was pure, unless nitrate of lead had been used in the adulteration; in this case the lead salt will be found on the filter. But if there is a whitish residue on the evaporating dish, this may be weighed and put down as so much impurity.

Mix a few particles of pulverized lime and some of the white residue together, and moisten the mixture with a drop of water. If nitrate of ammonia be present in this residue, it will be decomposed by the lime, and the fumes of ammonia will be set at liberty. The absence of all smell of ammonia shows distinctly the absence of an ammoniacal salt. In this case nitrate of soda may be suspected. This salt burns like saltpetre when thrown upon a piece of burning charcoal; and blotting paper impregnated with this salt in solution and dried forms touch-paper, which, when kindled, burns with a deflagrating noise, but without flame, until it is totally consumed.

Supposing the impurity is nitrate of lead, it will be found now as chloride of lead mixed with chloride of silver on the filter. Filter through the mixed chlorides dilute nitric acid for some time. The chloride of lead will be dissolved, and pass through the filter, leaving the chloride of silver on the filter. Evaporate the solution to dryness; if there be no residue, there is no lead salt mixed with the silver salt.

Having in this way satisfied yourself of the purity of the nitrate of silver purchased, proceed further as follows:

Take—

    Rain water   -   - 2 quarts or 64 ounces.
    Crystallized nitrate of silver   -   6   "

Stir the salt in the water until it is dissolved. This solution will contain a little less than forty grains of nitrate of silver to the ounce of water. Divide the solution into two halves.

IODIDE OF SILVER.

Take a drachm of this solution and add to it drop by drop a solution of iodide of potassium, as long as a yellow precipitate is formed; let the precipitate settle; then decant the fluid portion and wash the precipitate with a couple of drachms of water; let the precipitate again settle, and finally pour away the supernatant water. This yellow substance is *iodide of silver*.

Mix the iodide of silver with the one-half of the nitrate of silver solution and stir the mixture with a glass rod. After standing for an hour, filter this solution and then add it to the other half.

Now, throw a small piece of blue litmus paper into the solution and let it remain a quarter of an hour. If the color does not at all change to red in this time, or but *exceedingly slightly*, the bath will be in a proper condition to receive the collodionized plate. On the contrary, if the blue color almost immediately becomes red, this is a sign that the bath is much too acid; and you have now to neutralize it with carbonate of soda, or oxide of silver. Such an occurrence, however, will seldom be met with, for pure nitrate of silver is a neutral salt, that is neither acid nor alkaline; and an impure salt you will reject at the very outset. Still we will indicate the means of correcting this acid condition where it does exist.

CARBONATE OF SODA.

The easiest method of neutralizing a bath is that with carbonate of soda; because oxide of silver is but very feebly soluble in the cold solution. Dissolve a drachm of carbonate of soda in a small quantity of

water, and add of this solution drop by drop a sufficient quantity until the acidity is completely neutralized. The bath must be well stirred after the addition
of a few drops of the alkaline solution, and then tested.

OXIDE OF SILVER.

Take a drachm of the nitrate of silver solution and
add to it drop by drop a solution of caustic potassa as
long as a brown precipitate is formed; finally, allow
the precipitate to settle, and pour away the liquid on
the top. Mix with the precipitate a couple of drachms
of water, stir the mixture well, and again allow the residue to subside. Decant again. Repeat this operation of washing two or three times; and at the end
separate the brown powder from the supernatant
liquid—this is *oxide of silver.*

Mix the still moist oxide of silver with the acid bath,
and stir it up well; boil the mixture, and then set it
aside for a number of hours. The free acid combines
with the oxide and forms with it a silver salt, which
probably is nitrate of silver; and the bath thus is rendered neutral. The bath solution is again filtered.

It is quite an advantage to set a funnel aside always
for this special purpose of filtration; in this case it is a
very easy operation to filter the bath every evening, or
every week, according to the work done or the liability
of the bath to receive dust and other impurities. The
filtering paper may be used over and over again re-
peatedly until it finally gives way by some mechanical
rupture. Never be afraid of injuring the silver solution by filtration, as some have insinuated; the view
is erroneous; on the contrary, you avoid numerous

troubles by always preserving the bath free from all mechanical impurities.

The bath, which may be either of glass, photographic ware, or porcelain, is placed in an inclined position in the dark, or non-actinic room; in this room the albumenized plates are coated with collodion, and then directly immersed by means of a porcelain or glass dipper in the silver solution.

Each bath ought to be furnished with a cover or lid to keep out both dust and light both during the operation of sensitizing and at every other time. In immediate proximity with the bath it is advisable to fix a glass funnel dipping into a receiver beneath. This funnel must be a permanent fixture, and is intended to receive the sensitized plate the moment it is taken out of the bath. The plate rests in the funnel quite easily without any danger of the collodion film being injured by coming in contact with the sides of the conical shaped funnel, a thing that is impossible. In this position the excess of nitrate of silver drains from the plate and is collected in the bottle beneath, from which, from time to time, it can be returned to the bath.

As soon as the plate ceases to drop any more of the silver solution, it is immediately transferred to the plateholder for the subsequent operation of being exposed.

But we have not yet finished with our discussion of the bath solution. It is liable to get out of order; and it is necessary to know how to remove the troubles that may occaisonally supervene.

The bath is most sensitive when it is in a neutral condition, but in this condition the collodion film is apt to be fogged all over the surface in the subsequent operation of development with the ordinary iron developer; with the collo-ferric developer this trouble of fogging is not likely to occur. Whenever the film becomes fogged a drop or two of nitric acid have to be added to the bath solution, and so long but cautiously added until the evil is removed. We mean by fogging that the film becomes covered with a veil or cloud, as it were, which renders it all over slightly opaque, even after the fixing of the image, or the removal of all soluble iodides. But the most frequent cause of this fogging is not to be attributed so much to the bath as to the careless manner of exposing the plate during the time that it is being sensitized, or after removing it from the bath to the plateholder, to diffused actinic light. Such a plate is exceedingly sensitive; and a very small amount of common light will suffice to produce a great deal of damage in a very little time. Therefore, before any attempt is made to doctor the bath with acid, see first that your light is in a proper condition of non-actinism. Of this we shall speak in a special chapter.

By repeated and long use the bath solution becomes impoverished and deteriorated by impregnation with foreign substances—substances introduced with each plate and produced by chemical decomposition or otherwise. Thus let us examine what the collodion film contains on its introduction into the solution. In the first place, there is the collodion itself containing pyroxyline, alcohol, and ether, and in addition, sometimes, the results of the partial decomposition of both ether and alcohol, as well as impurities in the soluble cotton itself, as, for instance, free sulphuric acid or an alkali. To these may be added the bromo-iodized salts used in the photographic collodion. Thus, then, the bath will gradually be rendered impure by dilution with alcohol, and ether certainly, and with other substances, such as sulphuric acid and an alkali, probably. But by the chemical decomposition which takes place immediately, when the collodionized plate is immersed in the solution, we have, in addition to the above nitrate of ammonia, nitrate of the oxide of cadmium and other soluble nitrates, produced according to what salts may be found in the bromo-iodizing solution.

Now each collodionized plate introduces a little of each and nearly of all of the ingredients enumerated, on all occasions, certainly, a little alcohol, ether, and of the soluble nitrates. These, by their gradual accumulation, must have a tendency to put the bath out of order and render it less efficacious than at the beginning, when newly prepared. But by the mutual action of nitrate of silver on each of these, or on each other, other compounds are produced. The photographer, therefore, will no longer be surprised that the silver bath does get out of order ; in fact it would be surprising if it did not.

But now the question arises: How can these troubles be removed? or, if incapable of being removed entirely, how can they be diminished?

Mechanical impurities, such as dust and collodion, and insoluble chemical precipitates or crystals, such as the iodide of silver, bromide of silver and sulphate of silver, can be easily removed by careful and frequent filtration.

Volatile liquids, such as ether and alcohol, are diminished to a minimum quantity by boiling or distillation; by the latter method they may be collected in a receiver and applied afterward to some useful purpose.

If iodide and bromide of ammonium were alone used in the bromo-iodizing solution, the salt arising from double decomposition in the silver bath would be nitrate of ammonia; this salt might be removed entirely by fusion and decomposition by heat, after the bath had been evaporated to dryness, and nitrate of silver would remain. But collodion seldom, if ever, contains these two salts alone, and consequently all other resulting nitrates would remain in fusion along with nitrate of silver.

It is hence apparent, that an old bath cannot be freed of its salts except by the decomposition of the silver salt itself, and furthermore, that filtration and distillation are the only means within our power of making an approximation to the purification of the silver bath.

Cyanide of potassium has been recommended as a sure means of restoring a disordered bath; it is quite certain that by dropping into the bath a drachm or so of the solution, then by placing the bath in the sun for several hours, and afterward by filtration, the silver bath becomes momentarily wonderfully improved, but it soon loses this quality and becomes finally worse than it was before this treatment.

Upon the whole, it is advisable, after an old bath has been used for a long time, and has been several times boiled and subjected to distillation, to precipitate the silver by means of a solution of common salt, to wash and dry the residue, and finally reduce the resulting chloride of silver to the metallic state by fusion. But the operator will find no advantage in doing the work himself; there are silver and gold refiners who buy up all such residues of silver and of gold, and make a business of reducing them. Nevertheless, we shall devote a special chapter to this department of a photographer's business, to which the reader is referred.

CHAPTER IV.

THE department, upon which we now enter, is a subject of the most vital importance, and at the same time the least understood, and consequently the least under control. It has baffled the attempts of many an author to describe, because it is a department of art as well as of science. A combination of art and science can alone solve the difficulties.

The first aim of the artist in painting is to obtain a natural roundness and an agreeable contrast of light and shade in his portrait; these properties not only confer vitality to the inert picture, but at the same time this vitality is sparkling, as it were, and pleasant to behold.

This ought also to be the first aim of the photographer.

In order to attain to this desideratum the artist manipulates with his lights so long, not by guess, but in accordance with the science of optics and of taste, until his model is so placed as to present in person the artistic model he wishes to copy.

The photographer must do exactly the same.

Let us here then present before our readers some general principles. Place a globe on a pedestal and let it represent the sitter's head. Let us suppose we wish to make a picture of this globe so that it shall appear perfectly flat like a round table—how must the globe be illumined so as to give the appearance required?

Shut out all the light except the one immediately in front of it; or let the sun shine directly upon the surface to be copied.

The globe itself will appear flat—and so will the picture, because the illumination is apparently equal all over the surface.

By what means are *solid* objects depicted on a *flat* surface so as to appear solid?

Firstly, by the conveyance of the lines of contour of the given object to a given point or to given points; and

Secondly, by shading the object more and more according as the part becomes more and more distant.

Hence, if there is no difference in the illumination of a given object, there will be no contrast of light and shade, and consequently the picture will be in like manner devoid of light and shade, and consequently *flat*.

Can the globe be placed in such a position as to be illumined most in front and then that the light gradually becomes less intense to the edge of the illuminated hemisphere?

Remove the globe back from the window; and suppose the window to be a small opening at the end of a long corridor, which, when this opening is closed up, would be quite dark; and let the ceiling, the side walls, end, and floor be covered with black woolen cloth. Then it will be evident by experiment, that, as the globe is made to recede, its surface gradually will assume more and more apparent roundness to the eye of the beholder; and this apparent roundness will be improved until finally there is a balance between the light and shade. If the globe be carried further back, the balance will be destroyed by a preponderance of darkness or shade. Thus, too much light, or too little light, is equally opposed to the production of apparent solidity in an object.

Instead of having an opening in the corridor at the end, let this be closed up, and another be opened right above the globe in the ceiling; and let the eye of the spectator be placed on a level with the center of the globe. What will be the phenomenon in this case?

One-quarter of the globe alone will be visible, and the most illuminated portion is that part which in reality is the most distant, and the nearest part; that is, the part nearest the eye, receives the least amount of light; and thus, what one part gains in luminosity, it loses in distance, and *vice versa;* so that here also the idea or appearance of solidity is destroyed. With such a light we should have the same result, however distant the light might be removed from the globe, as long as the eye preserves its position on a horizontal level with the center of the globe.

We hence deduce, in general terms, that a vertical light is altogether inferior to a horizontal light for the illumination of an object, that is intended to be so shaded as to appear solid when photographed, the eye or the lens being supposed to be in the horizon of the center of said object.

We deduce, furthermore, that a horizontal light, when the light and the eye are in the same plane, will, under all ordinary circumstances, produce a flat picture, because it suffuses the object with an equal quantity of light all over its surface.

But, if neither a single vertical, nor a single horizontal light, unaided, will produce the proper illumination of an object so as to exhibit the right contrast of light and shade, that shall cause apparent solidity, what is to be done?

We must avail ourselves of every aid that presents itself; and such aid may be derived from a *combination* of lights, direct or by reflection; thus, in the case of the vertical light above mentioned, the eye in its prescribed position could distinguish only one-fourth of the sphere illuminated; now let us arrange a large white screen near the globe at an angle of forty-five degrees with the floor, its central part being as high as the center of the globe, we shall perceive a much larger part of the globe illuminated than before; and yet the light has not been changed either in its original direction, in quality or in quantity; but we have manipulated with our light, and made it subservient to our wishes.

But we might have accomplished the same object by admitting a small quantity of light from an aperture, and allowing it to arrive at the globe in the same direction as that which was reflected.

What we here present are general principles; and from these general principles it is required to elaborate a system of lights and reflectors (screens), by means of which the sitter may be artistically suffused with an agreeable contrast of light and shade.

As soon as the operator has once found out a position for the model, and an arrangement of curtains and screens in a given room, which will produce the best effect of light and shade, he can ever afterward fix his model and reproduce his arrangements. All this is very easy; but in case a group has to be photographed, he will frequently be greatly perplexed unless he makes himself quite familiar with the general principles which we have endeavored to inculcate.

With these few hints we will now proceed to the sky-light, etc., which form an essential part of a photographic establishment.

As a general rule the photographer's glass-room is found in the upper story of a building, and in such a position that the adjoining buildings are not higher, and where there are no trees, steeples, or chimnies to cast shadows upon the roof.

The best position of a house for this purpose is when the roof runs directly East and West; still it is possible to get along with any direction, and to fix or construct the lights accordingly.

Taking then the normal condition, in which the roof runs East and West, the floor of the garret is removed, in order to allow the sky-light to be as far remote as possible from the sitter. Upon the side of the roof which inclines to the North the sky-light is to be constructed, and continued, after it arrives at the eaves, until within a couple of feet of the floor. The distance from the East and West walls must be from twenty to thirty feet at least. In this case half the width of the roof either on the East or West side can be devoted to the sky-light and side-light, both, of course, looking North. Curtains are arranged in parts with pulleys and cords, so as to cover both of these windows entirely or partly according to circumstances. It is well to have two sorts of curtains, one set opaque so as to shut out the light altogether, and the other set of blue or white semi-transparent material intended simply to modify the light.

In an ordinary sized building, three-fourths of the whole flight is devoted to the glass-room, the remaining portion being set apart for other purposes, such as dark-room, printing, or store-room, etc.

If the roof of the building runs North and South, and said building is isolated from other edifices, a sky-light is constructed on either side of the roof, and the Northern end, at least, a portion of it, is devoted to the side-light. These three windows are all furnished with movable opaque curtains or screens designed for excluding the direct light from the sun when in the East or in the West, or portions of light in certain directions.

The plans which we have described are such as may be followed, when the building is already constructed; but little alteration is needed in the general form of the original construction, and consequently the expense will not be very great; but if we had to construct a model glass-house, our plan would be different from the preceding. The Southern half of the upper part of the house we would devote to the posing-room proper, the background being placed near the South wall, whilst the sitter looks toward the North. Along the middle of the other half an alley is constructed for the camera. A general idea of the outer form of our model glass-house may be given by imagining two boxes placed endwise in contact, but one of them being

twice as high as the other. The tall one represents the
posing-room, the low one the gallery for the cameras,
in connection with each other. On the roof where the
two parts join the sky-light is constructed, having an
inclination of forty-five degrees; and on either side
there is a side-light to within a couple of feet to the
ground. All these lights are furnished with curtains
and opaque shutters. Only one side-light is used at a
time in portraiture. On either side of the avenue devoted for the camera, are side-rooms for various purposes, such as toilet-rooms, stock-rooms, dark-rooms,
etc. The intention of this arrangement is to keep the
camera in as dark a place as possible, in order that the
space between the camera and sitter may reflect but
little light into the lens; for it is impossible to obtain
a bright picture on the ground glass when the space
referred to is full of light; there is no contrast; in fact
in such a case, where your room is full of light, you
would be taking a picture of the atmosphere rather
than of your sitter; and your work would always be
unsatisfactory.

Illumine your sitter but not your room!

The glass employed for such lights is, when all
things are considered, the ordinary strong and colorless crown glass. With a convenient and proper arrangement of curtains and blinds, there is no particu-
lar advantage, if any at all, in having the windows
glazed with blue stained glass, ground glass, or glass
painted either of a dead blue or white. These all more
or less obstruct actinic light, and there are times when
all the light, that can possibly be obtained, is required.
Still we must guard the reader against supposing that

negatives are good according to the quantity of light
that has access into the gallery; the truth is frequently
just the contrary; that is, a very small amount of light
frequently will produce a better picture than an un-
limited quantity.

The walls and ceiling of the glass-room must be
painted of a dead bluish-gray color, or a gray-drab;
and the floor must be covered with a carpet of similar
colors. The backgrounds are made of woolen cloth, or
some material in imitation of woolen cloth. One side
may be gray, and the other white; or separate backgrounds may be used each of a different shade. Pic-
torial backgrounds in monochrome are sometimes very
appropriate; but the operator must always bear in
mind that in portraiture the background is a secondary matter, and must not be made the most prominent
part of the picture. By placing the background more
remote from the sitter, it will be more out of focus and
less distinct in the picture; with this knowledge the
artist can arrange the background so as to produce the
effect required.

In addition to the backgrounds, a number of swing
screens covered with white cotton cloth are required
to be used as reflectors. For, supposing the model is
placed with his back nearly South-West, and his face
looking North-East, it is evident that a portion of the
right side of his head and face will be too much in the
shade. To obviate this defect a screen is placed at
some distance South of the sitter and facing the North,
and at such an angle as to reflect a sufficient quantity
of light to relieve the deep shadows on the side of the
face in question.

2*

The sitter must be placed back toward the South side, and far enough to escape the vertical rays from the sky-light, otherwise the upper part of the head will be illumined disproportionately with the rest of the body; and large shadows will be produced beneath all the prominent parts of the head and face, as the nose, eyebrows, cheekbones, etc. The tendency of such a light will be also to flatten the head in the picture, as we have already mentioned in reference to the illumination of a globe.

In fine, place the sitter so that there are no deep shadows on the eyes, beneath the nose, or on the neck; let there be only one reflected star on each eye; this can be effected by means of the curtains; let one side of the face be slightly more luminous than the other, the brightest parts being those which are most anterior; let the eye of the beholder, or the lens of the camera be a trifling distance above the elevation of the eye of the model; if it were otherwise, the opening of the nostrils would be quite visible and unpleasantly depicted in the picture. Place the sitter in a comfortable, easy, and natural posture; and when accessories are to embellish the picture, such as a piano, table, etc., let them be appropriate to the sex, profession, or condition. It is absurd to attempt to make a fitness of things where it was never intended; it is a constraint that makes a picture ludicrous.

CHAPTER V

THE lenses used in portraiture, are all, or nearly all of them, constructed after the same formulas. In a work like this, which is designed for the practical operator, it would entirely be out of place to discuss these formulas, which are intelligible only to the physico-mathematican. Such lenses are called portrait or compound lenses to distinguish them from lenses of apparently a much more simple construction which are used in landscape photography.

The anterior part of the portrait combination consists of two lenses cemented together with Canada balsam, which makes them appear like one lens. The first or outer lens is constructed of crown glass, and is double convex; the inner lens is double concave, and of flint glass. It is easy to distinguish these two sorts of glass: flint is colorless, or if slightly tinged it is with that of a very faint yellow; but crown glass a faint greenish hue. Remember, the convex part faces the sitter.

In the middle of the tube and between the two lenticular combinations is found what is called the diaphragm or stop, being a piece of blackened brass with a central aperture. In some portrait combinations the stops are movable and are furnished with apertures of different diameters. The intention of these stops is this: the central and the peripheral part of a lens produce pictures, it is true, independently of each other, but not at the same distance from the lens. This property can easily be verified by sticking a round disc of leather upon the central part of a lens and then focussing some object on the ground glass. The picture in this case is formed by the glass ring external to the leather disc. Now remove the disc of leather, and place upon the lens in its stead a piece of leather as large as the lens, but of which the central portion was the disc previously. In this case the light passes only through this central part. Focus again the same object upon the ground glass. You will find you have to increase the distance between the lens and the ground glass, or that the focus for the outside or central portion of a lens is longer than that of the external or peripheral part of a lens. Hence, it is impossible, under ordinary circumstances, to obtain a sharp picture of an object with the full opening of a lens; for points and lines that are out of focus become converted into surfaces; and we see that if we focus with the central part of the lens, the rays that come to a focus from the outside part will form their sharp picture in front of the ground glass. In consequence of this, stops are used for excluding all the peripheral rays; and the smaller the aperture in the diaphragms the sharper the picture. But there is a limit to this advantage; the aperture may be so small as to allow but little light to pass through it, and, although the picture that is thus formed is very neatly defined, it is but very faintly luminous; but luminosity produces photographic or chemical action on the prepared plate; and this action varies in magnitude with the quantity of light; so that when the luminous picture on the ground glass is faint, it will fail partially or totally to produce any impression on the chemically prepared surfaces. In landscape photography, when the condensation of light is very great, the smallest aperture may be used; whereas, in the glass-room, there is but a small surface, comparatively speaking, that transmits its light through the lens, we are obliged to use the largest stop.

The posterior lens is also a combination of two single lenses, but these are not cemented together. The inner one, that is, the one next after the diaphragm consists of flint glass; it is concavo-convex in form, the convex side looking toward the center of the tube. Between this and the last lens there is a small brass ring which keeps the two lenses apart. The last lens is a double convex lens, but the inner surface is more convex than the outer one. The reason of this variety of lenses, so as to produce a working combination, is not intelligible to any one who has not made the subject of optics an earnest study. You have seen that the peripheral parts of a lens act differently from the central parts in converging rays to a focus; and that diaphragms are applied to remedy the evil; now you must proceed a step further and learn that, when light passes through a lens, whether convex or concave, it undergoes a change in passing through; before it entered, it was colorless; now when it makes its exit, it is *colored*. Another step teaches us, that lenses made of one sort of glass have the property of correcting the color produced by a lens of another sort of glass. Thus the light that passes

through the front double convex lens of *crown* glass
becomes colored by this passage ; but the double concave lens of *flint* glass, being placed immediately behind it, receives the colored rays and restores them
partially to their original colorless condition. Other
combinations succeed in order, whose function it is to
complete the restoration, and still allow a residual
quantity of convexity of surface to remain in order to
converge the rays as they finally pass out; for without
convergence there can be no picture.

For landscape photography the same sort of lens
can be used as for portraiture; but one of less costly
construction will answer the purpose equally well ; it
is also much lighter in weight, and hence more portable. Many of our portrait combinations are so arranged that the front lens can be used singly for landscapes, whilst the two are required for portraits. In
such combinations, the back lens is not so much regarded as a corrector of the front lens, but as an addi-
tional lens which shortens the focal length of the combination, and hence produces a greater condensation
of light which is capable of making the photographic
or actinic impression on the prepared chemicals, and
which a single lens would be incapable of effecting.

The view lenses proper are found in the market
under various forms; those of Jamin consist of a single
combination of two simple lenses cemented together
with Canada balsam. Several others are of the same
construction. The stop or diaphragm is placed in
front of the combination, and the latter is generally
turned right round, so that the lens which is posterior,
when it is used in portraiture, becomes placed in front

for landscapes. But, as before remarked, a combination of two lenses can never be made to correct the whole amount of decomposition of light; hence, such view lenses, although in many instances exceedingly excellent, have not the same reputation as combinations of three simple lenses so as to form triplets, which, when the formulas are properly calculated, and the curves carefully ground in accordance, can correct the decomposition more effectually than a doublet, in the ratio of two to one. The simple lenses of such a triplet may be either cemented together as one lens, or combined according to some optical principle at given distances apart. The view lenses of Dallmeyer and Ross, made in this form, are equal in every respect to the very best in any country, and by many photographers they are regarded superior to all others.

The Globe lens is a very happy combination of two pairs of compound meniscuses, which, when mounted, are in the form of a globe. The stop is in the middle between the two compound meniscuses. The corrections for both the spherical and chromatic aberrations are nearly perfect; and the angle of view is very large; it is a very favorite lens among our American photographers. Dallmeyer's wide-angle lens will perform all that the Globe lens can do, and has the advantage of using more light.

The Steinheil periscopic lens is in fact a Globe lens, consisting, however, of two simple meniscuses of the same sort of glass; it is mounted like a Globe, with a central stop. The chromatic correction is effected in a very curious way, which has hitherto not been recognized by opticians as possible. The angle of view in this combination is also very large; but its action is said to be very slow; and on that account it will scarcely ever compete with the Globe and the Wide-Angle lens.

The Orthoscopic combination is another form of lens which may be used for taking views. It consists of two combinations of two lenses each. The angle of view of this form of lens is much more contracted than that of the Globe or the Wide-Angle lenses of Ross and Dallmeyer ; it derives its name from the fact, that straight lines in a chart or map are exhibited straight or orthoscopic in the copy. But the Globe or the Wide-Angle lens will also do this orthoscopic work more quickly and to a greater extent. The optical construction between the Globe and the Orthoscopic lens is quite different; so much so that the former may be said to be corrected with positive or convex lenses for both spherical and chromatic aberration; whilst the latter is corrected with negative or concave lenses.

The lenses from abroad which have gained the highest reputation here are those of Voigtlander, Ross, Dallmeyer, and Jamin; but we do not need any longer to avail ourselves of foreign aid in this respect; the portrait combinations of two or three of our native opticians in this country, for instance those of Willard & Co., Am. Optical Co., Chapman & Wilcox, and Roettger cannot be surpassed for accuracy of workmanship; and the Globe lens for copying and landscape operations stands pre-eminent.

CAMERAS.

There are various forms of cameras according to the purposes for which they are intended. The requisites in a camera are that it shall be rigid and yet light; the ground glass must be perpendicular to the optical axis of the lens, and its motion must be even and always remain perpendicular to the axis. In large cameras the ground glass has two motions, a quick and a slow motion, by which the focussing can be easily effected without touching the lens itself. This is convenient. For taking card-pictures the camera is generally constructed so as to allow the plateholder to slide into different positions by means of which several pictures of the same sitter can be taken on the same plate. If, moreover, there are two or four lenses on the same camera, and the plateholder also slides, a still larger number of pictures can thus be taken at the same sitting.

Stereoscopic cameras are always constructed for the reception of two lenses of equal power; but with a sliding plateholder stereoscopic negatives can be taken with a single lens. In this case, however, the camera must also be made to slide into a position two inches and a half either to the right or the left of its first position after the first exposure, according to whether the right side picture was taken first, or the left side picture.

Cameras are now manufactured with such a degree of perfection, that it is needless to enumerate the troubles that photographers had to expect in former times.

Above all things, however, ascertain at the outset whether the ground glass and the negative glass are exactly at the same distance from the lens. To do this, put a plate of flat glass into the holder and draw the slide. Lay a straight and flat ruler over the edges

of the frame and measure the height of the upper side
of the ruler from the surface of the glass below; move
the ruler about over different parts of the surface and
measure the height. If this height remains the same all
over the surface of the glass plate, it is an evidence that
the glass corners have been accurately set. Now lay
the ruler over the frame of the ground glass, in different parts, and measure the corresponding height; if
these are all the same, and also correspond exactly with
that of the negative glass, the construction of these
two parts is correct and accurate.

TO MAKE THE ACTINIC FOCUS AND LUMINOUS FOCUS
COINCIDENT.

It may happen that, however accurately the ground
glass and the sensitized plate may coincide in distance
from the lens, and however correctly you may have
focussed, yet the picture on the negative is not as sharp
as the picture on the ground glass. This is caused by
the non-coincidence of the actinic focus and the luminous focus; that is, the compound lens has been either
over-corrected or *under-corrected*. If a lens has been
perfectly corrected, all the rays of the spectrum come
to a focus at one and the same point ; in an un-
corrected and under-corrected lens, the blue, that is,
the actinic rays come first to a focus; whereas in an
over-corrected lens the luminous rays are brought first
to focus.

The actinic focus is the focus of the picture on
chemically prepared paper.

The luminous focus is the focus of the picture on
the ground glass. Hence, if the lens has not been
sufficiently corrected, the luminous picture on the

ground glass will be more distant than the actinic picture on the sensitized plate; and it remains for you to find out by actual experiment how much the difference of distance is. Put in a piece of cardboard between the edges of the ground glass and the flange upon which it rests, and try if this improves the picture on the sensitized plate ; if this has improved the result but not completely cured the defect, add another thickness of cardboard until you have overcome the difficulty.

But if the lens has been over-corrected, the ground glass must be gradually sunk deeper in its frame until the desired correction has been attained.

Secondly, see that there are no pinholes or screwholes by which light can find access into the interior of the camera, excepting through the lens.

See, too, that the spring valve of the plateholder opens and closes accurately when the slide is put in or taken out.

Whenever accessories have to be taken together with the portrait in the picture the camera must be horizontal ; for if it be tilted, perpendicular objects are tilted also, and will be represented as such in the picture. But when the portrait alone is taken, it is customary to raise the back of the camera, so that the lens is inclined downward in order to look down upon the sitter. In this way a position can be found where every part of the model will be nearly all in focus.

To focus with ease and accuracy it is better to have a large opaque cloth tacked to the front frame of the camera all round the top and the two sides, and sufficiently long as to cover the head and shoulders of the operator whilst he is examining the picture on the ground glass. A pair of good spectacles will also be found exceedingly useful in making the focus quite sharp. It is customary to bring the eye of the sitter into accurate focus. This can easily be done, for the inner corner of the eyelids is a very visible object.

See that the head rest is nowhere visible, nor anything else that ought not to be seen. Place the sitter so that almost every part of his body is nearly at the same distance from the lens. To do this the model must sit sidewise, turning his head to the front. Let the position be graceful, easy and natural. If any part, such as the hand, or knee, etc., be too much out of focus, let the position be changed until the picture is satisfactory. Adjust the robes, ribbons, ringlets, etc., of your sitter, which do not flow or sit in artistic forms, and direct your model to regard some small and easily seen object, by which the eyes are in no way constrained nor the face forced into a stare. When all is thus adjusted, put the cap on the lens, remove the ground glass and substitute the plateholder containing the sensitized plate. Draw out the slide and wait a moment to allow the camera to be quite at rest. Your model must now regard the prescribed object; take off the cap from the lens and count the seconds.

It is always an advantage to have a clock furnished with a seconds' hand, in sight from your present position, so that you have no trouble with your watch;

and the spectacles that you use to focus with, had always better be left in a given place in or near the camera, for it is too much trouble to put them in your pocket and then have to take them out again when wanted.

Close the cap and the slide. Carry the plateholder into the dark room.

CHAPTER VI.

In former times the room in which the pictures were developed, the plates sensitized, etc., was properly called a dark-room—it was dark, gloomy and disagreeable. It is no longer so now. From discoveries that have been made, this developing room may be the lightest room in the establishment, as long as the light is of the proper color. Let the window of the room be glazed with orang-red colored glass, and in addition fix up a curtain of thin red woolen cloth or flannel. The light that passes through this window exercises no action upon the sensitized plate; you may develop the plate in front of this window without any danger of fogging the impression. But be sure to shut up every avenue to *white* light; the smallest beam of this light is detrimental to your success; the light that comes through the keyhole is injurious.

This room ought to be called the *non-actinic* room, because the light with which it is suffused is non-actinic, which means, that it has no action on prepared chemicals.

It is well to try the efficacy of your non-actinic room by experiment. Sensitize, therefore, a collodionized plate, and then expose it to the light which enters through the orange-red window for two or three minutes. Pour on the developer in the usual way. If the plate does not change color in the least, it is an evidence that actinic light, at least, has not made any impression upon it, and you may then, with full confidence, afterward perform all your developing operations with ease and certainty.

To facilitate the operation still further, we always prefer developing by the aid of a light which comes from below, and thus shows the progress of development by transmitted light. For this purpose let the developing corner or table be a projection beyond the wall of the building, and let a large square of nonactinic glass be glazed in an aperture on the top of this table; this pane can admit light only from below upward.

During development the plate, whether large or small, may be held, it is true, between the thumb and finger, but it is much easier to hold it supported on a pneumatic plateholder. In this position you can cover the plate with the developing solution with the utmost facility. It requires some experience before you can flow the developer evenly without any stoppage or interruption; the operation must be quick, and yet it must not be violent, otherwise much of the developer will rush off at the opposite side, and carry with it much of the free nitrate of silver which was still on the plate, and which is so very beneficial in producing intensity. If the developer proceed slowly over the exposed film, the development will be uneven, one part being already out before the other has commenced. If the developer stop and refuse to proceed in a given direction, there will assuredly be found in the finished negative a dark line or curve at that place, which will be very offensive in the print.

Furthermore, if the developer be poured from a great height (and we regard two or three inches high in this experiment), its momentum the moment it comes in contact with the collodion is sufficient to wash off the impressed silver from this part, and to produce, in consequence, a very weak patch at this spot. To avoid all these troubles, and especially with a large plate, we prefer laying it at the bottom of a dish of gutta-percha at one end. In this case, the dish being slightly tilted, the developer can be poured into the opposite end in sufficient quantity to cover the plate the moment it is again raised to a horizontal position or tilted in the opposite direction. This is a very effectual plan of development, and, especially so, if the dish has a transparent bottom, for then you can watch the development by transmitted light.

A transparent developing dish is constructed in the following manner : Take a thin piece of hard and well dried wood, four or five feet in length, one inch wide, and half an inch thick, and plane a groove along the middle about three-sixteenths of an inch deep, sufficiently large to allow the edge of an ordinary pane of glass to slide along it. Four lengths are then cut out so as to make a rectangular frame, the ends being cut in a miter-box at an angle of forty-five degrees. A pane of glass is then tightly framed in the groove; and the frame is firmly nailed together. After this is done, a cement consisting of five parts of resin, one part of beeswax, and one of red ocher are melted together, and when fluid a sufficient quantity is poured along each seam or groove all round on either side, and along all the corners. After the cement has set, the excess is pared off and polished down smooth with a red hot pointed piece of metal. The frame is finally covered with a coat of varnish, made by dissolving sealing wax in alcohol, in a teacup, over the stove. Coach or any other varnish will answer the purpose. We have a set of such frames, of different sizes, for the different sized plates in use. Each transparent plate is at least two inches longer than the plate to be developed; the excess of length is the part which is to receive the force of the developing fluid as it falls out of the vial which contains it. If the plates to be developed are very large, the dish that is to hold them may be constructed so as to have two projecting handles, either screwed on to the ends of two parallel sides, or formed out of these two sides themselves, which are left projecting some four or five inches beyond the ends. The dish and plate are then easily supported by the two hands, whilst an assistant pours on the developer.

CHAPTER VII.

THE image on, or in the collodion film, after exposure, is a latent or invisible picture of the object upon which you focussed; by the application of certain chemical solutions to the collodion film, the image, before latent, gradually emerges from its prison-hold into being. Such chemical solutions are called developers; these act like all other chemical substances that produce reductions or decompositions. Thus, if we add a solution of iodide of potassium to another of bichloride of mercury, a color, a beautiful scarlet color, starts out from the previously transparent and colorless fluids; we have no power, no knowledge whatever, that will enable us to tell *a priori*, the result of the admixture of two unknown solutions simply from their appearances, but if we know the solutions we do know with accuracy the result of such an admixture, because this result is simply that derived from previous experimentation. But, notwithstanding a very extensive accumulation of facts, we are still in utter ignorance, and probably shall for ever remain so, as to the true cause of chemical action; why, for instance, the salts of the protoxide of iron are green, whilst those of the peroxide are red; why hydrosulphuric acid produces, yellow precipitates with a salt of cadmium or of arsenic, an orange-red precipitates with antimony, and a black one with so many of the salts of other metals.

We do not know what the precise action is; be it the result of electricity, of light, of heat, of gravity, which institutes some physical change in the ultimate atoms or molecules that constitute the new compound. And just as ignorant are we, for the experiments are very similar, of the rationale of the development of the latent photographic image. We know simply that a protosalt of iron, as well as other chemical substances, has the property of reducing the salts of silver and of gold to the metallic state, and that, if the protosalt contain at the same time some organic material in admixture, the reduction will be complex, partly reguline and partly a compound; and we know furthermore, or suppose, at least, that light institutes some peculiar physical changes in the silver solutions, whereby they become predisposed to undergo this reduction on the application of the reducing agent. This is the extent of our theoretic knowledge at present. Here we stop on this subject, and proceed at once to the mode of developing a negative.

Prepare in the first place the following solution:

DEVELOPER.

Protosulphate of iron - - -	1 ounce.
Rain water - - - - -	16 ounces.
Acetic acid - - - - -	3 "
Alcohol - - - - -	$1\frac{1}{2}$ "

Pulverize the salt, mix it intimately with the liquids until dissolved, then filter and preserve in a stoppered bottle for use.

We give the above formula in preference to any of the more modern formulas which contain more or less of gelatine, which is twofold in its action: it modifies the color of the developed image and acts at the same time like an acid in restraining the development.

The developer being poured upon the plate carefully and quickly so as to cover the whole of its surface almost instantaneously, and still retaining whatever silver solution may have remained on its surface, you keep the plate in motion so as to mix up the developer thoroughly and to cover every part of the collodion film. If the picture starts out almost at once, the plate has been exposed too long; on the contrary, if a minute or half a minute expires before any change is produced on the film, the exposure has been too short. If the change, of which we speak, begins the moment the developer comes in contact with the collodion, and continues slowly but distinctly, the exposure has been about right.

The great art of development is twofold : it consists in knowing when to stop, and to stop in all cases before or as soon as fogging commences. Fogging is the reduction of the silver solution into the reguline condition even where light has not acted, thus producing a veil on the parts that ought to be transparent. It will frequently take place when all the solutions are freshly prepared. Any saccharine or gelatinous substance mixed with these solutions, that is, with either the silver bath or the developer, has a tendency to prevent the silver from being reduced in those parts upon which light has not acted. Acids have also the same effect ; it is on this account that acetic acid is found in the developer, and nitric acid in the silver solution. Much of the troublesome effects of fogging, too, may be avoided by understanding the extent to which the plate may be sensitized, and also by covering the plate with a substratum of albumen as recommended in a previous chapter.

For instance, as an experiment, drop a little of the bath solution upon a plain glass surface, and add to it a little of the developer, the experiment being performed in the dark room ; reguline silver soon begins to make its appearance on the surface of the glass, and thus to destroy its transparency. This is an example of pure fogging. But if the glass has been previously albumenized, the same amount of fogging will not take place, the albumen prevents the silver reduction, or at least restrains it. You see then one of the benefits of coating the plates with albumen previously to coating them with collodion.

It would appear from this circumstance that the naked glass surface has a tendency to institute the silver reduction, the moment the developer comes in contact with it ; and hence it may be inferred, that if we can prevent the solutions from coming in contact with the glass surface, we shall at the same time restrain reduction and consequently fogging. This analysis of the subject teaches us how long to sensitize the plate. As soon as the collodionized plate is immersed in the bath the nitrate of silver solution begins to permeate the collodion film, and at the same time to produce by double decomposition the iodide and bromide of silver on the surface and in the substance of the collodion. This decomposition is made manifest to the eye by gradual whitening of the film. Naturally the front surface of the collodion film becomes first white, then the middle, and finally the whole film to the glass is of a cream-white. But by a careful observation you may hit upon the exact time when the outer or front surface of the collodion film is cream-like in color, whilst the back surface, or the surface which is next the glass is of a slight bluish tinge. This indicates that the silver solution has just permeated the film as far as the glass. Now is the time to take the plate out of the bath and to expose it; that is, to expose it before all the soluble iodides and bromides are decomposed. These lie between the free nitrate of silver and the surface of glass, and thus prevent or restrain the reduction of the silver salt into pure silver; they prevent fogging. But should fogging take place before the picture is thoroughly developed, or, at least, before the shadows are sufficiently opaque, your best plan will be to wash the plate immediately and then to fix the image and deepen the intensity afterward by what is called redevelopment or intensification.

Another method of proceeding in such a case consists in washing the plate thoroughly, then in pouring over it a dilute solution of either bromide or iodide of potassium, and allowing it to remain on the surface a short time. Naturally such a solution decomposes all free nitrate of silver in the collodion film, and free nitrate of silver is the main condition of fogging. Now this being removed, wash the plate again, and pour the developer again upon the plate and watch proceedings. Gradually all the detail of the picture is brought out, and the picture apparently is complete, regarded simply as a picture, but the lights, shades, and middle tones are all there in regular gradation; but as a photographic negative it is yet incomplete; the opaque or dark parts are not yet sufficiently dense. Hold up the negative and place your fingers between the negative and the light ; if they are distinctly visible through the shadows of the negative, the latter are not yet dense enough. You must proceed with the development. Previously pour off the old developer, wash the film and then flow it quickly with the following solution:

Nitrate of silver - - - - 36 grains.
Rain water - - - - 3 ounces.

Pour away all excess of the silver solution from one corner, and then cover the film with fresh developer. This proceeding will seldom fail to make the shadows sufficiently opaque for the printing operation. Take the plate out to the light, hold it up to a tree, and see if the leaves are visible through the dense shades; if not, the development has proceeded far enough. The plate may now be thoroughly washed and immersed in the fixing bath.

But should it happen that the development cannot be carried on to its completion without fogging being the result, wash the film and fix the image, which is supposed in other respects to be perfect, and is only lacking in intensity.

FIXING SOLUTION.

Cyanide of potassium - - 4 drachms.
Water - - - - - 10 ounces.

Pour the solution over the plate and keep it in motion; the yellow and cream-like parts will soon become transparent, and the picture will now appear much more beautiful than before. As soon as all the unaltered iodides and bromides have been dissolved by the fixing solution, wash the plate on both sides and until every trace of the cyanide has been removed.

This washing, like all the preceding operations of the same nature, may be performed at a jet of water issuing from a tap at the end of a water-pipe inserted in a barrel, or being the termination of the ingress of water from the public water works. There is no danger of the collodion film being torn off the plate by means of the current of water if the surface of the plate has been previously albumenized ; but the film may easily slide off, if there has been no substratum, by the manipulations of a novice, but not so in the hands of an experienced operator. Of course your aim will be to learn by experience and finally to become perfect in this beautiful art.

INTENSIFICATION AND TONING OF THE IMAGE.

Supposing that the picture possesses all the detail and gradations required, but that the shades are not sufficiently dense, you may flow the plate whilst the film is still moist with the following solution :

Terchloride of gold -   -   - 2 grains.
Water - - - - - 4 ounces.

Whilst the negative is still moist pour a sufficient quantity of the above solution over the film as to cover it quickly ; the tone will change very rapidly becoming more of a blue-black ; if kept on, however, too long a retrograde action sets in, and the tone gradually becomes fainter. Watch the opportunity when the whole picture has assumed its first bright blue-black tone; then pour the excess of gold solution back again into the stock bottle. This solution soon becomes exhausted, which is easily known by the disappearance of the yellow color of the terchloride, and must then be replenished with some fresh salt. The double salt of gold and sodium, or gold and potassium is well adapted, but not that of gold and lime.

Wash the negative and place it upon a leveling-stand with water on its surface.

The following stock solution is next required :

Fill a four ounce vial with rain water and throw into it an ounce or more of bichloride of mercury, shake the mixture well and set it aside to dissolve; take care to keep at the bottom of the bottle some of the undissolved salt, by which you recognize that the solution is concentrated. Label the bottle: Concentrated Stock Solution of Bichloride of Mercury. Place side by side with this a bottle of acetic acid. These two stock solutions are required to make the following mixture for present use:

Concentrated solution of bichlo-
    ride of mercury   -   -   - 1 drachm.
Acetic acid   -   -   -   - 1   "
Water   -   -   -   -   - 6 drachms.

This mixture is now poured upon the moist plate; hold the latter in such a position as to let the light pass through it from beneath; you can then easily observe the gradual darkening of the film, and stop the action when the intensity is satisfactory. By this means you can get any amount of opacity in the shades, and the tone of the negative is very pleasing to behold.

3*

The only disadvantage it possesses, is the expense of the gold solution; after all, this is a subordinate consideration, as long as the work is good. Should the expense be an objection to the above intensifying process, we give the following which we formerly practiced and have found quite reliable. Make the following stock solution:

TINCTURE OF IODINE.
Stock Solution.

Iodine	-	-	-	-	-	40 grains.
Alcohol	-	-	-	-	-	1 ounce.

SOLUTION OF IODINE FOR PRESENT USE.

Of the stock solution	-	-	10 minims.
Water	-	-	-	-	-	1 ounce.

Where it is convenient, take the moist negative and, holding it where the sun can shine upon it, pour a sufficient quantity of the Present use solution all over the film, and oscillate the plate so as to keep the solution in motion. The tone of the negative will soon assume a faint rose color, whilst the solution itself has gradually lost all its color, the iodine having been taken up by the silver in the shades of the picture. It is better to have the Present use solution quite dilute in order that the deposit may be free from granulation. Wash the plate and place it on the leveling-stand. Prepare the two following stock solutions :

STOCK SOLUTION OF PYROGALLIC ACID.

Pyrogallic acid	-	-	-	-	24 grains.
Acetic acid	-	-	-	-	2 ounces.

STOCK SOLUTION OF NITRATE OF SILVER.

Nitrate of silver   -   -   - 60 grains.
Rain water   -   -   -   - 2 ounces.

Now take of the first solution half a drachm, water four drachms, and mix with this solution two or three drops of the solution of nitrate of silver. Add as little silver as possible, as long as the solution gradually increases the opacity of the shades, when poured upon the negative ; for a rapid action can easily be instituted, but the deposit will be pulverulent and gritty. The slower the action, the more uniform and smooth the film becomes. As soon as the proper amount of intensity has thus been obtained, the negative is very thoroughly washed and then placed on the leveling-stand for the subsequent operations.

CHAPTER VIII.

TO VARNISH NEGATIVES, AND TO PREPARE NEGATIVES FOR THE
SOLAR CAMERA, AND FOR COPYING WITH THE CAMERA.

WE have now described the method by which a good
negative can be prepared for the ordinary printing
operations upon paper. The only thing that now remains to be done with this negative, is to coat it with
some varnish or other preservative material, by which
the film is protected from injury in the subsequent
manipulations. Most of the varnishes in the market
become tacky when exposed to the direct rays of the
sun during the hot days of Summer; the paper then
adheres to the collodion film in patches, and tears them
off when it is removed from the plate. But a film of
albumen is free from this trouble, and we recommend
it as a very practical and reliable mode of coating
negatives. A single coating in general is sufficient;
but two coatings are better.

Separate the whites from a number of eggs, and
beat them up well. Then make the following mixture:

The white of egg, well beaten	- 10 ounces.
Distilled, or pure rain water	- 5 "
Ammonia - - - -	- 1 drachm.

Pour a sufficient quantity of this solution upon the moist
film of the negative, so as to cover it completely; remove
any particle of dust or other concrete substance by means

of a corner of a piece of paper, and then allow the excess of albumen to drain off. The plate is now put away on the drying-rack to dry. When dry the film may be coated a second time, if this operation be deemed necessary, taking care to pour the albumen upon the end of the plate opposite to that on which it was poured the first time, and to place the plate on the drying-rack, also, in an inverted position.

The albumen solution, above prescribed, will keep for an indefinite time.

VARNISH FOR NEGATIVES.

Some may object to this mode of protecting the collodion film, and prefer keeping to the old system of coating the film with varnish; we, therefore, give a single formula for preparing a suitable varnish for the purpose.

VARNISH TO BE USED ON THE COLD DRY PLATE.

Gum sandarac - - - -	2 ounces.
Oil of lavender - - - -	1 "
Alcohol - - - - -	14 "
Chloroform - - - -	3 drachms.

Allow the materials to digest in a warm place; when the gum is dissolved, the clear portion may be decanted off for use when required.

This varnish is poured upon the negative in the same manner as collodion, the excess being allowed to drain back into the stock bottle; remove all particles of dust, and then rear the negative away on the drying-rack to dry.

The negative is now complete and ready to be handed over to the printer; but before we proceed to give instructions about printing, it is our duty to describe how to prepare negatives suitable for camera printing or printing with the solar camera; this sort of printing is quite distinct from what is denominated contact printing, and requires a negative considerably different from that which we have just described.

SOLAR CAMERA NEGATIVE.

Take the thinnest plate glass compatible with the manipulations which it has to undergo; coat it as usual with a very thin film of albumen, taking, for instance, one ounce of the stock albumen solution as given in this chapter, and diluting it with eight ounces of water. Filter the solution. Be exceedingly careful to get an even film, perfectly free from the slightest particle of dust or insoluble material. Put the plate away to dry in a clean place where there is no dust stirring.

COLLODION FOR A SOLAR CAMERA NEGATIVE.

Take the collodion as prepared by one of the preceding formulas according as it is for in door or out door work, and dilute it in the following manner:

Bromo-iodized collodion - - 1 ounce.
Alcohol - - - - - 4 drachms.
Ether - - - - - 4 drachms.

This collodion, of course, will be very thin and can be flowed over the plate without producing the slightest reticulation.

The film is sensitized in the usual way and in the ordinary silver bath in every day use. Expose the plate somewhat longer than you would for a negative for contact printing; that is, the exposure must be complete; for an under-exposed plate is not to be thought of in solar camera operations.

How are you to know when a plate is under-exposed or over-exposed?

Take, for instance, a picture of the trunk of a tree, its branches and leaves. If the plate be under-exposed, you will get no detail, none of those beautiful indentations, rough prominences and peculiar markings on the bark, which are as characteristic of the tree as the different forms of wool and hair are to the animal; you will obtain, also, none of the nerves and fibers that distinguish the leaves. Your negative will present, develop as long as you like, nothing but outlines of the trunk, branches and leaves of the tree in the midst of thick darkness—your negative is totally devoid of detail.

An over-exposed plate, on the contrary, goes too much in the opposite direction, and the development is so rapid that the detail of the indentations, prominences, markings, etc., becomes soon annihilated by being clogged up with too much deposit, and all the diversity of light and shade is finally indistinguishable; the picture is one mass of fogginess, like a meadow covered with mud after a freshet—it is all mud.

The middle way between these two extremes is the one we take or strive to get into when we expose properly; but for our present purpose, it is better to slightly over-expose than under-expose, because our object is to get all the detail rapidly, so as to preserve the negative quite thin in the shades.

The same developer may be used as before recommended, adding a drop of nitric acid to each ounce of the developer. As soon as the picture is thoroughly out in detail everywhere, wash the negative immediately, for a step further is always an injury to the working qualities of the plate; avoid making the shades opaque.

Your negative, if right, will be a sort of phantom negative, constructed upon gossamer, very thin, finely delineated, and very beautiful. Wash it well, and put it away on the drying-rack to dry. Negatives for the solar camera must not be varnished; in fact, there is no need of any varnish, for the film is not subjected to any hard usage; but it must be kept thoroughly out of the dust.

Whilst developing and washing a negative it is advisable to receive all the wash water in an appropriate vessel beneath; from time to time a handful of salt is thrown into the fluid at the bottom which converts the soluble nitrate of silver of the washings into an insoluble powder, which will gradually accumulate at the bottom. There will be in addition a quantity of pure silver mixed with it, produced by the action of the protosulphate of iron on the free nitrate of silver on each plate. At a distance of five or six inches from the bottom of the vessel there is an outlet pipe into the sink which carries away all excess of fluid. This pipe can be opened and closed at will by means of a stopcock. It is well to keep it closed during the operation of development; that is, in the day time in order to allow the requisite decompositions to be effected by the salt solution, as also during the night in order that the insoluble chloride of silver and the reduced silver may settle to the bottom. Early in the morning and before operations commence the stop-cock is then opened and the surplus water is allowed to flow away. The pipe is again closed, and a little more fresh salt is thrown into the vessel. If you are doing an extensive business you will be surprised how much silver you have thus saved by the end of the year.

Negatives for making transparent positives, such as glass stereographs, which are so universally and deservedly admired, and negatives for making opal or porcelain pictures by means of the copying camera, are all prepared in the same way as those for the solar camera. You may, it is true, obtain positives from your *ordinary* negatives, but they will be far from satisfactory; they will in general be mere black and white daubs; there will be no, or seldom any, detail.

We apply this mode of preparing negatives for copying purposes to the preparation of transparent positives for producing enlarged negatives. Thus, for instance, a properly prepared quarter-sized negative of some choice landscape, taken on the spot with the dilute collodion, is placed in the copying camera, and a plate coated with dilute collodion is placed at the opposite end of this camera to receive the impression, which, of course, will be a transparent positive. Follow the rules above given and give rather more than the full exposure and stop the development the moment all detail is visible. Wash and fix with cyanide of potassium in the usual way. Finally, wash thoroughly and dry the positive. This positive, if carefully prepared, will be sharp, semi-transparent, bright looking, and full of all the minute delineations of the original from which the negative was taken, and, if also carefully preserved, will be the nucleus or model from which any amount of negatives may subsequently be taken, of the same size or of any given size required. There is no branch of photography that tests the skill of the operator, and the perfection of the lens more than this sort of reduplication; but, at the same time, there is none which is more interesting and remunerative.

Suppose now we wish a negative of the landscape above mentioned and of which we took a quarter-sized negative for copying purposes; all we have to do is place the small transparent positive in the copying camera and to arrange the conjugate foci by means of the two sliding bellows so that the picture on the ground glass is of the size required. A globe lens, or one of Dallmeyer's lenses, is the most appropriate for the purpose. If you wish a negative for ordinary printing operations, you must use the undiluted collodion and pursue the common routine of development. You can, we maintain, in this way get an enlarged negative as good as if you were to take an original negative of this size on the spot; in fact, it is possible, you may get a superior negative, because of the troubles always arising out of the transportation of a tent, etc., for work of this size.

Before we leave this subject of the wet negative and its development, we may put in a few remarks about the fixing solutions. In many large establishments the negative is fixed in a solution of hyposulphite of soda, and a large bath, holding two or three gallons of the fluid, is always kept in readiness.

FIXING SOLUTION WITH HYPOSULPHITE OF SODA.

Hyposulphite of soda	-	-	-	2 ℔.
Rain water	-	-	-	2 gallons.

Fresh hyposulphite can be added to the bath every two or three days; and it will be well to filter the solution at least once a week, and at the same time to collect the deposit, which is a sulphide of silver, as a separate silver residue for reduction. This bath is very convenient in a gallery, for the negative can be left in it for a long time without being materially injured; but from our experience both in opal printing by the wet process, as well as in the fixing of dry plates, we are *convinced* that an old and much used fixing solution is frequently the cause of much fogging and stains on the plate, and we therefore prefer a *fresh solution* for each plate; and we furthermore prefer fixing with cyanide of potassium, to fixing with hyposulphite of soda, although the former is a very poisonous material and acts with so much energy as to obliterate the picture itself, unless great care be employed in its use. The poisonous effects can be entirely avoided by using the pneumatic holder for developing and fixing, etc., the plate; and a quick eye can designate the exact moment when to stop the fixing; the operation is quick and effectual.

Pyrogallic acid is also used sometimes for developing the image; it is an excellent developer and produces a very beautiful picture, but its action is not so

rapid as the iron developer. The deposit on the plate
is of a different nature from that produced by the iron
salt, being a compound silver salt containing organic
matter, whilst that from the iron solution is mostly reduced silver. The exposure must be longer with pyrogallic acid than with the iron salt.

PYROGALLIC ACID DEVELOPER.

Pyrogallic acid -   -   - 12 to 18 grains.
Acetic acid   -   -   -   - 1 ounce.
Water   -   -   -   -   - 7 ounces.

In Winter as much as eighteen grains may be used
to the ounce of acetic acid, whilst in Summer twelve
grains will be found quite sufficient.

We cannot leave this subject without adverting to
the excellent developer with gelatine and protosulphate
of iron, the discovery of M. Carey Lea, Esq., to whom
we are indebted for so much that is valuable in photography. His formula is as follows :

COLLO-PROTOSULPHATE OF IRON DEVELOPER.

" Add an ounce of sulphuric acid to three ounces of
water, and set aside to cool. Then add to this liquid
an ounce of good gelatine; let it swell and dissolve,
placing it for that purpose in a slightly warm place,
not exceeding blood heat, for twenty-four hours. Then
add iron filings in excess, avoiding all application of
heat; let it stand for several days. Finally, add half a
drachm of acetate of soda and filter. Dilute the solution to fifteen ounces."

Many modifications have been made of this formula
but with very slight emendations, if any. With a
proper length of exposure the picture can be developed

to the requisite intensity without any other aid. If photographers were patient chemical manipulators they would always use this developer or some modification of it; we ourselves never think of using any other, and yet we have not recommended it as the developer proper for the operator, because—because he would blunder somewhere in its preparation, fail to get good results, and condemn both us and the ferro-gelatine developer to the abode of Hades, literally, the Kingdom of Darkness.

CHAPTER IX.

THE operator might as well pick rags, tear them into fibers, make them into pulp and finally convert them into paper, as to put himself to the trouble of preparing his own albumen paper. This is now a business of itself, and it is fortunate that it is so; for it is quite a bore and an expense to prepare any chemical or mechanical article in small quantities for home consumption.

Nevertheless, we will tell our readers how the paper may be prepared. The paper suitable for photographic purposes must be quite uniform in texture, smooth on the surface, perfectly white, free from all metallic salts, and as far as possible impermeable to fluids. It is to be hoped our paper manufacturers will experiment to a greater extent than they have done, so as to attain to this impermeability without at the same time impairing the flexibility of the paper. The requisite paper being on hand, the next thing is to sensitize it for photographic purposes. The ordinary process consists in mixing the chemical ingredients with a solution of albumen, and then to let the sheets of paper float on this solution for about three minutes, after which they are taken out and hung up to dry.

If we had to prepare photographic paper, we would do it in the following manner :

The paper should first be floated on a solution of

gelatine of the proper consistence, hung up and dried.

Secondly, each sheet should be passed between a pair of rollers, on a highly polished plate of steel, in order to fill up the pores of the paper with the gelatine.

Thirdly, let each sheet float about three minutes on a solution of alum which converts the gelatine into a sort of leather, rendering it insoluble, and, to a much greater extent than before, impermeable to fluids.

These three operations are quite preparatory to the really photographic part of the business. The sheets when dry are now ready to be floated on the prepared albumen.

Take the whites of any number of fresh eggs and beat them up for a long time, that is for an hour or two so as to disintegrate the substance, and break up its adhesion. Allow the albumen to settle. Then prepare a mixture according to the following formula :

Clear albumen	-	-	-	20 ounces.
Distilled water	-	-	-	6 "
Ammonia	-	-	-	-	2 drachms.
Chloride of ammonium	-	-	6 "

Instead of the chloride of ammonium, the same amount of chloride of sodium, or of the chloride of barium may be used. Beat the solution again well together, or shake it well up in a bottle ; after subsidence the clear portion is poured into a large flat bath. The paper, prepared as above directed, are floated on the gelatine side next to the albumen; each is left for three minutes on this solution, taking care previously to break up all bubbles with a glass rod. The sheets are then taken out and hung up to dry in a room quite free from dust. When dry, two sheets placed back to back are put between two highly polished plates of steel and passed between rollers, and then packed away for sale or use.

The film of albumen contains a soluble chloride, which, when it comes in contact with nitrate of silver, is converted into chloride of silver, a salt which is very sensitive to light.

Albumen paper must be kept in a dry place, otherwise it is liable to change. The different tones in samples of albumen paper manufactured by different houses, arises in a great measure from the chloride which is used; thus, chloride of ammonium communicates to the print, when it leaves the printing-frame a reddish tone, whilst the salt of sodium or of barium inclines more to the black. This difference of color, however, in the original print, is not of material consequence, since, by toning afterward in the gold solution, the final hue is the same or nearly the same, whatever chloride was used in the preparation of the paper.

SENSITIZING OF ALBUMEN PAPER.

The soluble chloride in the albumen paper must first be changed into the insoluble chloride of silver, before the paper is ready for receiving any impression from light. For this purpose we again require, as in the preparation of the negative, a silver bath. The vessel which contains the silver solution is a flat dish of photographic ware, porcelain, glass, or varnished wood. Large porcelain dishes are made on purpose to receive the silver solution; but owing to the expense some photographers construct wooden dishes of thin dry wood, which answer the purpose quite well. Along the edges they pour a melted solution of wax and resin, or a solution of sealing wax or lac in alcohol. The latter solution is the better of the two and is easily made. A proper quantity of sealing wax is broken up into pieces, and put into a teacup containing alcohol; the cup is then placed on the stove and stirred about until the solution is made. A proper quantity of this solution is poured along the edges and seams, and is rubbed quickly in by means of a brush. This cement soon dries. The solution may afterward be considerably diluted and used as a final varnish to the inside and outside. The inside will require two or three coats of varnish in order to render the wood watertight.

SENSITIZING SOLUTION.

Nitrate of silver - - - -	2 ounces.
Water - - - - -	14 "
Alcohol - - - - -	1 "

This bath contains about sixty grains of nitrate of silver to the ounce of the solution. The intention of the alcohol is to prevent blistering in the albumen film, and consequently where there is no such tendency the alcohol may be omitted. A small quantity (about a drachm) can be added to the bath every time you are about to sensitize a fresh quantity of paper; at the same time you may also add a drachm or two of crystals of nitrate of silver. This bath is placed in the non-actinic room in a convenient position near a wooden partition; near the bath and along the partition an inclined gutter is constructed of well varnished

4

tin plate, and so placed as to allow any fluid that drops into it to drain into the silver bath.

The sheets of albumen paper are sensitized in the following manner : The four corners of each sheet are bent from the albumen side back to the extent of half an inch, thus forming four vertical projections, by which the sheet can be seized by two opposite corners diagonally. When so held, and the hands are brought slightly nearer together than the width between the two corners, it is evident the middle parts of the sheet will hang down. The albumen surface is below and is convex. In this position the sheet is lowered upon the silver solution, which has just previously been filtered, the middle part thus coming into contact with the fluid first, the two sides are gradually let down, until the whole sheet lies flat upon the solution. By this means you avoid the production of bubbles. Still it is always better to be quite certain as to this head; raise each corner, therefore, separately by one of the four ears, and examine the parts for bubbles; if there are any they must be broken up by means of a glass rod kept close by for the purpose. If the paper is apt to cockle or refuse to lie down upon the solution, breathe upon the back part, it will immediately yield to the impression of the moist breath and fall down. As soon as the sheet is all right and every where in contact with the nitrate of silver, you may allow it to remain for *one minute;* after which you raise one of the corners by means of a piece of strong silver wire, and then lift the sheet gradually up from the fluid, and you then pin it or otherwise attach it by clamps to the wooden partition behind, and just so high as to allow the lowest diagonal corner to drain into the bath which lies close to the partition. When the sheet is large or of the full size, it is well to pin the *two* upper corners and one of the lower corners to the partition, but still so that the sheet hangs as it would do, if supported only by one corner. The lowest corner is not pinned, but dips over the side of the bath.

Another sheet is now placed upon the sensitizing solution in the same way; and the excess of silver solution from the first sheet having drained off by this time, this sheet is now transferred to another position on the partition, where the lowest corner can just hang over the gutter at its farthest extremity. Here it is left to dry completely. The second sheet takes its place after draining, as before, next in order to the first; and so you proceed to the last sheet. If a drop of silver solution still adheres to the lowest corner of each sheet, remove it with a bit of blotting paper.

Old filtering paper, through which solutions of silver have passed, pieces of blotting paper used for this purpose above mentioned, spoiled sheets of sensitized paper, clippings of prints, in fine, any paper whatever which contains stains of silver, have to be preserved in a large chest or barrel kept for the purpose; in a short time we will tell you what to do with them.

As soon as you have done sensitizing the paper for the day, empty the silver solution into the stock bottle. At the bottom of this bottle we always keep a layer of chloride of silver, and the stock bottle itself retains its position in the dark-room. The chloride of silver is obtained from an old silver bath by throwing into it a solution of common salt, as long as any white precipitate is produced. The vessel is then set aside for an hour or so in the dark-room, after which the supernatant solution is easily separated by decantation from the residue beneath. After which the chloride is washed with pure water by shaking and again allowed to subside; the operation of decantation and washing is performed twice; all the water is finally poured off and the sensitizing solution may then be poured upon it and kept there until again required for use.

The object in view by keeping the silver solution in contact with chloride of silver is to keep the sensitizing fluid always colorless, a method which has answered our purpose exceedingly well. When the chloride itself becomes colored, dry it and preserve it for reduction with other silver residues at the proper time.

When the sensitized sheets are *perfectly dry*, they may be submitted or not submitted to the fumes of ammonia, just as you feel inclined about the matter. The advantage of fuming is, after all, not very great; and the finished print is equally good whether the sensitized paper was fumed or not. Paper that has been fumed is probably more sensitive, and thus requires less exposure. The simply sensitized paper, when dry, may be preserved for some time without changing color, or deteriorating; but if it has been once fumed it soon becomes yellow; the fuming, therefore, must take place only a short time before the paper is required for printing.

FUMING OF SENSITIZED PAPER.

This is a very simple operation. A large cupboard may be made out of a drygood's box by placing it on one end and fixing it on a frame as high as the knees, or about two feet high. The lid is fixed on hinges so as to open sidewise. The sheets of sensitized paper are then fastened with a pin at each corner around the three sides and on the door or lid, as also on the upper end, taking care in every case that the albumen film looks outward. At the bottom of the box a saucer is placed; into this saucer, after it has been made warm over the stove or a spirit lamp, a few drachms of ammonia are poured; and the door is then closed. The ammonia soon evaporates and comes intimately in contact with the albumenized surface. In ten minutes or a quarter of an hour, the door is opened and the sheets are taken out and hung up to air in the dark room, of course. They are then ready for use.

THE PRINTING OPERATION.

There is a great variety of printing-frames in the market; and it is a difficult task to say which is the best for general purposes. Some of them have special advantages for vignetting which the others do not possess; and in this case there can be no difficulty in making the appropriate selection. Since you will require a number of printing-frames, especially for card-pictures, you will do well to get one of each different make and then select that which suits you best, before you purchase a complete outfit.

The negative is placed in the printing-frame, collodion side uppermost; the sensitive paper of the proper size is then placed upon the negative, so that the collodion film of the negative and the albumen film of the paper lie in contact; over the paper comes a piece of

soft cloth, either loose or attached to the spring back
which is pressed down tightly so as to keep the paper
in close apposition with the negative, and fixed there.
The printing-frame is then turned up and placed so
that the direct rays of the sun or diffused light can
pass through the negative to the paper.

By means of the folding door at the back of the
frame you can, from time to time, examine the progress
of the actinic impression; this examination must take
place, however, in very subdued light, otherwise the
purity of the whites would be injured. Very soon the
picture will appear quite perfect as a picture, but it is
not yet perfect for the purposes intended; you must
over-print, print until the shades begin to be bronzed
by the action of the light, and the whites are no longer
quite white. The prints are then taken out and stored
away in a drawer or between the leaves of a book until
you have finished printing for the day or for the occasion.

The next operation is performed in a very weak light
or in the non-actinic room. It consists in cutting the
prints to the proper size for mounting. For card-pictures there are punches and machines that do the
work very effectually and quickly. The one made by
Wm. B. Holmes, Broadway, is excellent. If you have
neither a punch nor a machine, the next best is to cut
out a piece of glass of the required shape and size, and
then to grind the edges perfectly smooth and even.
You may then place this piece of glass on the print,
and holding them firmly together in the left hand, you
may easily clip the edges off with a pair of long scissors

all round the glass; this is the easiest process next to that with the machine.

Another method is to lay the print on a sheet of plate glass, and to place the glass form over it; you may then proceed round the edges of the glass with a sharp-pointed penknife and cut of the edges of the paper as you proceed. For such work as this it is well to have a table so constructed that the top can revolve on a pivot like a potter's table. So provided you can easily keep your fingers firmly fixed on the glass form and, at the same time, revolve the table so as to bring each side of the glass into an easy position so as to make the next incision in succession.

Similar glass forms are used for stereoscopic and other prints of a small size; but larger prints may be cut out with a square to the size desired.

All the clippings are preserved in the chest or barrel above mentioned.

We prefer cutting the prints out at this early stage, because we save a large amount of gold in the toning operation, by simply toning no more than is needed. This is quite an important precaution, whose value you will soon learn to recognize.

Let us now proceed to the next operation in succession. The cut prints are all thrown into a vessel of pure rain, or well water, in which they are kept in motion in order to facilitate the separation of all the free nitrate of silver; the sole object of the washing is to do this. Where the convenience exists, a stream of running water is allowed to flow over them; but where it does not exist, the prints are transferred to another vessel of pure water, whilst the water in the first vessel

is allowed to enter by means of a pipe and tap into
another containing a solution of salt. The nitrate of
silver is thus converted into the insoluble chloride
where it is afterward collected either by filtration or
subsidence. The water from the second vessel, containing the prints, also enters the one which contains
the solution of salt, in order to collect what little nitrate of silver may still have remained in the prints
after the first washing. After the prints have thus
been thoroughly washed, of course in the dark-room,
they are transferred to the toning bath, which is a
large flat dish sufficiently capacious to hold the ordinary quantity printed in your establishment.

The toning solution consists essentially of the terchloride of gold; all other substances are secondary in
importance; and the terchloride of gold is an article
which you can seldom obtain in a pure form, or in an
invariable form. It is sold in general as a double salt,
either the double chloride of gold and sodium, of gold
and potassium, or of gold and calcium. If you deal
with only one photographic establishment, you may,
probably, always obtain the same sort of gold salt, and
thus produce in general the same uniform results every
time you have to tone. This is the only salt which it
is well for the photographer to prepare himself; for
then he knows its composition.

TO PREPARE TERCHLORIDE OF GOLD.

Pure gold can be obtained from the mint; and frequently a sufficient quantity of pure scraps of gold can
be met with at the dentist's; in case of need the gold
coins of the country may be used; they contain, how-

ever, an alloy which will detract in a trifling degree
from the purity of the salt thus obtained and from its
effects in toning.

Make a mixture of two ounces of hydrochloric acid
and one of nitric acid; this forms what is called *aqua
regia*, or royal water, from the fact that it is capable of
dissolving the noble metals gold and platinum, which
are insoluble in either acid alone.   The truth is that
these metals are dissolved easily enough in chlorine,
and it is probably the chlorine, which is produced by the
mixture of the two acids, that performs the operation.
Place the mixed acids in an evaporating dish on a water
bath, and throw a quantity of pure gold leaf and scraps
into the mixture, and keep adding as long as they are
dissolved; finally, with some gold still remaining undissolved at the bottom of the vessel, evaporate the liquid
to dryness, or allow it to evaporate spontaneously to dryness in a large wash-basin exposed to the sun's rays.
The solution must not be evaporated to dryness at a
temperature greater than that of boiling water, otherwise the salt will be decomposed.   As soon as the salt
has thus been made dry by either artificial or spon-
taneous evaporation, it is still an acid salt; that is, it
contains still a small quantity of free acid, which you
must decompose.   Dissolve, therefore, the resulting
reddish colored salt in an ounce of water and add to
it powdered chalk as long as an effervescence is produced.   As soon as this ceases, pour off the liquid portion from any undissolved carbonate of lime (chalk),
and evaporate it to dryness again on a water bath.
You have now got the double chloride of gold and
calcium; and if you always prepare it by the way pre-

4*

scribed, it will always have the same uniform composition, from which you may reasonably expect to get
uniform results when toning.

PREPARATION OF THE TONING BATH.

The double chloride of gold and calcium	4 grains.
Acetate of soda	80 "
Water (one quart)	32 ounces.
Alcohol	1 ounce.

The bath is best when prepared the day before it is
required; but it may be used the moment it is made.
More gold may be added if needed, which you will
have to determine from the slowness of the action.
Warmth materially hastens the toning operation.
Rapid toning, however, is not to be recommended.
Keep the prints in motion, and turn them round from
time to time ; if they are allowed to rest in one place,
irregular patches of toning are apt to be formed, which
cannot be removed or equalized afterward. You will
gradually see the change in tone as it proceeds. As
soon as the color is a brilliant purple, and before the
slate blue sets in, remove each print into a vessel of
pure water, until the toning operation is complete.
You will naturally understand that the prints have to
be washed, toned, and fixed in the non-actinic room,
because, until they have been fixed, they are still sensitive to the action of the light and thus liable to
change.

If you aim to get *bright, brilliant,* and *uniformly well-
toned* prints every time, it is advisable to prepare a
fresh toning bath for each operation of toning. You

will have, therefore, to learn by experience the quantity of gold required for a given number of prints, and thus to proportion the bath to the quantity of prints on hand. After toning, the residual gold solution is poured into a vessel for the purpose, containing a solution of the protosulphate of iron, which reduces the gold out of the solution in a pure metallic form; but the solution contains in addition, nitrate of silver, so that the precipitate produced by the protosulphate of iron is a mixture of gold and silver. When the precipitate has settled, the liquid is allowed to filter off, and the vessel is then again ready to receive the next supply.

After a time the sediment is taken out, thoroughly washed in several waters, and then treated as follows: Pour upon the sediment a sufficient quantity of dilute nitric acid (half nitric acid and half water) so as to cover it well; then heat the mixture to a boiling temperature and allow it to cool gradually. By this means the silver is dissolved, but the gold remains unchanged. Separate the fluid portion from the gold residue by filtration, and wash the residue to remove every trace of the nitrate of silver. Finally, evaporate the liquid portion to the crystallizing point and set it aside to crystallize, or evaporate it to dryness. The resulting substance is either crystallized nitrate of silver, or the silver salt in the amorphous condition, either of which may be used for the preparation of the sensitizing solution for paper. The gold may be dissolved again in nitro-hydrochloric acid according to the method prescribed, and is then ready for the preparation of the toning solution.

The prints are now stirred about in the water, and

then transferred singly to the fixing bath which is made as follows:

FIXING SOLUTION FOR PRINTS.

Hyposulphite of soda -	-	-	6 ounces.
Water (one quart)	-	-	- 32 "
Alcohol -	-	-	-	- 1 ounce.

This bath may be used over and over again; but in this case more salt must be added every time the bath has to be used, and a little alcohol is also added. Alcohol prevents the albumen from blistering. It is advisable, too, to filter the bath after every operation of fixing; the residue that remains on the filter is chiefly the sulphide of silver, which must be preserved separately from other silver residues, because it may be reduced separately.

The prints are kept moving in the fixing solution for about a quarter of an hour; the tone of the prints generally change to a reddish hue when they are placed in this bath, but it is again restored by the time the fixing is complete; the white portions of the paper, after the tone has been restored, will be quite pure, not spotted or speckled, when viewed by transmitted light. At this stage the prints are removed from the fixing solution and placed in the washing-tank.

CONSTRUCTION OF THE WASHING-TANK.

It is supposed the operator is furnished with water from the water-works, or from a running stream. The tank is cubical in shape like a large drygood's box; the water enters at the bottom. Along the edges at the bottom there is a strip of wood fixed, two inches high and one inch thich; this forms a projecting ledge all around; on this ledge a frame of wood, on which is stretched an open sieve of hair or wire, rests. A number of prints are placed in a single layer on this sieve; a second frame rests upon the first; and the sieve of the second frame is also covered with prints; and thus any number of frames are piled one over the other until all the prints are placed in layers ready for washing. The uppermost frame is then firmly wedged in its place to prevent the others from rising out of their position. In addition there is a leaden tube bent into the form of a syphon, one end dips into the tank and reaches to within half an inch of the bottom, the bend passes through a hole in the side of the tank, which is two inches from the top, and made watertight by stuffing and cement. The other leg of the syphon is conducted into the channel that carries away all the refuse water of the establishment. The diameter of this pipe is larger than that through which the water enters, so that when the water reaches above the lead of the syphon, the latter begins to work and the water flows out of the tank faster than it enters; in a short time the tank becomes quite empty, when the syphon ceases to act until the tank is again filled. This mode of washing prints is very effectual, and after they have remained half a day or over night subjected to this operation, all the hyposulphite has been thoroughly removed from the prints, and then permanency is thus assured. Prints that have been thus treated manifest no change, no decay in the space of three years, and we doubt not, they are, in the common acceptation of the term, quite permanent.

THE DRYING-FRAME.

Construct a large rectangular frame, like that for a swing looking-glass, and cover it with a sheet of shirting or calico. Support it also like a swing looking-glass in a movable stand. This stand can be carried to any open window or door, or even into the open air when occasion requires. The swing-frame is then inclined to receive the rays of the sun, and at the same time the prints, which are placed side by side on the cloth stretched across. An extra covering of net work may be stretched over the prints to prevent them from being carried away by the wind. By this contrivance the prints soon dry and are kept clean. They are now ready to be mounted.

MOUNTING OF PRINTS.

Make a paste of starch, in sufficient quantity for the number of prints to be mounted, in the following manner : Beat ordinary starch into powder and then into a thin paste with a little cold water; finally, pour this thin paste into boiling water, stirring the mixture well all the while and adding to it until the composition is somewhat thick. Now remove the vessel from the fire or lamp and set it aside to cool. When cool it is ready for use. Place the print on its face and brush over the back a sufficient quantity of paste until the paper lies flat and is completely covered. The print is now transferred to the mount and pressed carefully and smoothly down in its right position. The mounts, with the prints on, are put aside to dry.

As soon as the prints are dry, the mounts are passed once or twice between the rollers, which removes all asperities, and gives them a complete finish as far as photographic manipulation is concerned.

CHAPTER X.

THE NEGATIVE BY THE DRY PROCESS.

THE aim of the photographer has long been directed to discover some quick and reliable process by which plates can be prepared in quantity beforehand, and then can be carried out upon the field, exposed where the landscape is attractive, again repacked and developed at home. Many processes have thus been discovered which are, all of them, reliable in a certain sense, but few of them are at the same time quick. The latter consideration is, however, of little importance, as long as the plate can be depended upon to produce a picture under the circumstances prescribed. The process, which seems to have given more satisfaction than the rest, is that discovered by Major Russell, denominated the Tannin Process. With the alkaline development, too, it is almost as rapid as the wet process, but with this mode of development the process is not quite as reliable as with the acid development. Without any further preliminary we will describe the process as we practice it ourselves.

THE DRY TANNIN PROCESS.

The plates are cleaned in the the usual way, and if they are to be put away in a changing box, it will be necessary to round off the corners, otherwise they might be obstructed in their passage in and out of the changing box and plateholder; they are coated, too, with a thin film of albumen in the usual way. The collodion, containing more bromide than iodide, is appropriate for this sort of work; and the bath may be fifty or sixty grains strong; still there is no absolute necessity to change the bath; the one that you use for the wet process will be suitable enough. Sensitize the plate in the usual way; and, when the proper cream-like color has been attained, take the plate out, drain it and place it in a wash-basin of pure rain water, collodion film downward, until another plate is coated and put in the silver bath. As soon as this second plate is in the silver solution, go back to the first plate, wash the back of the plate, move the plate backward and forward with an oscillatory motion, so as to get rid of as much of the free nitrate of silver as possible by this first washing. The plate is now transferred to a second wash-basin of pure rain water, where it is again oscillated about and washed; it is now taken out and allowed to drain for a moment and then a dilute solution of bromide of potassium is poured over it once or twice, the excess being returned to the stock solution.

SOLUTION OF BROMIDE OF POTASSIUM.

Bromide of potassium	- -	36 grains.
Water	- - - - -	3 ounces.

The object gained by flowing the plate with this solution is to convert whatever free nitrate of silver may still remain on the collodion film into bromide of silver; any nitrate of silver, that might be left in the film, would be detrimental to the good working afterward. The plate is now washed again at the tap, or in another wash-basin of rain water in order to remove the bromide of potassium, and finally covered with sufficient tannin solution to flow backward and forward all over the collodion film.

TANNIN SOLUTION.

Tannin - - - - -	150 grains.
Loaf sugar, or honey - -	150 "
Water - - - - -	10 ounces.

Alcohol, sufficient to dissolve the tannin.

Measure out the tannin, and add alcohol until it is completely dissolved. Then mix this solution with the sugar and water and filter through a moist filter. The tannin solution is quickly prepared by the method here prescribed; it must be kept in a well-stoppered bottle.

We always use a fresh solution for each plate, and pour the residue or excess into a vessel to receive it; but the plate may first be coated with the tannin solution which has already been once used, and then, after draining, with a small quantity of the fresh solution. After draining, the plate is reared on one corner on a piece of blotting paper folded into several folds, and left to dry in a dark cupboard or secluded shelf free from dust.

All these different operations of washing and coating the plate will not require more than two or three minutes; and by the end of this time the second plate will be sufficiently sensitized in the silver bath to be removed into the first wash-basin. These wash-basins are very convenient for the washing purposes, because the plate can rest on the four corners on the concave surface of the basin without any liability of the film being injured by friction. This method, too, of preparing the tannin plate entails no change or further outlay than that required in the wet process, as far as regards collodion and silver bath. The process is easy and reliable.

EXPOSURE OF THE TANNIN PLATE.

Tannin plates, when dry, are put into the changing box; there are two or three forms of changing boxes in the market, but the one constructed by the Am. Optical Co. in New York is, in our opinion, the best and most commodious. With a little ingenuity any photographer may construct one for himself both simple and effective and at a small cost. The intention of the changing box is to contain the plates so that light cannot reach them, and, at the same time, to furnish an easy method of transferring them to the plateholder and back again without allowing them for a moment to be injured by any access of light.

All that the photographer requires on a photographic tour, becomes reduced down to the three articles: camera, tripod and changing box, all of which may easily be carried in the hands, supposing that stereoscopic pictures have to be taken. Whenever, a charming landscape presents itself, the camera is mounted upon the tripod, and the picture is focussed. A plate is next transferred to the plateholder and exposed.

One pair of lenses which we use, requires an exposure of three seconds in a good light to produce a very satisfactory picture; with these lenses we expose a dry plate under the same conditions of light for full one minute; that is, if we develop the plate with the acid developer.   The exposure, therefore, for a dry plate is about twenty times as long as for a wet plate.   Another pair of lenses, the globe lenses, produce a good picture by the wet process in five seconds; and by the dry process we expose about a minute and a half.   The ratio in this case is nearly the same as in the preceding example.   With the alkaline developer much shorter exposures would be amply sufficient; thus half the time in either case would be quite sufficient.   In some instances you will find it necessary to make a short exposure, in which case you make a note of the fact in your note book and develop accordingly with the alkaline developer.   Most of our friends, who are successful workers with the tannin process, decidedly prefer the acid developer; we prefer it ourselves.

ACID DEVELOPER FOR THE TANNIN PLATE.

Prepare the following stock solutions:

No. 1.—Acid, Pyrogallic.

Pyrogallic acid	-	-	-	18 grains.
Acetic acid	-	-	-	1 ounce.

No. 2.—Nitrate of Silver Solution.

Nitrate of silver	-	-	-	30 grains.
Rain water	-	-	-	1 ounce.

When required for use, make the following mixture:

For present use.

Of No. 1	-	-	-	12 minims.
Rain water	-	-	-	3 drachms.
Of No. 2 -	-	-	-	3 minims.

The collodion film is first made wet with clean water, and the mixture is the then poured upon it so as to cover it. If the exposure has been right, the picture will gradually begin to increase in intensity. Do not hurry the development; let it proceed slowly. Should the picture flash out very rapidly, add more acetic acid to the developer, or prepare a new developer with only one drop of silver, and ten or twelve drops of acetic acid to twelve minims of No. 1, and three drachms of water. When the action is slow, add more of the silver solution. With patience you get all the intensity desired. When the picture is thoroughly developed, it has a rich, reddish tone, and is quite intense in the shades. Wash it well at the tap, and fix the picture in a *fresh* solution of hyposulphite of soda containing a little alcohol, which will prevent the film from blistering; be careful to fix the picture thoroughly; then wash with a bountiful supply of water, and examine it now in strong daylight. If you do not like the red tone in the negative, it is easily changed to a splendid purple-black, by treating the film with the gold solution and afterward with the acid bichloride of mercury, as recommended in a previous chapter, under the head "Intensification." But you will find it more advantageous to leave the negative red, because this color is, comparatively speaking, non-actinic.

If the pyrogallic were acidified with citric acid, that is, if citric acid were substituted for acetic acid in all the preceding manipulation of development, the finished negative would have a bluish-black tone instead of the reddish tone; and if nitric acid and gelatine were substituted, the tone would be of a grayish-black. It is thus evident, that the acid used as restrainer, modifies the tone of the picture.

ALKALINE DEVELOPER.

Flow over the exposed plate dilute alcohol, containing equal portions of alcohol and water, and then pour back the excess, and wash off the apparent greasiness produced by the alcohol. Next pour over the plate the following solution:

> Carbonate of ammonia - - 1 grain.
> Water - - - - - 4 drachms.

Pour the solution back again into the vial, and add to it four minims of the following solution:

> Pyrogallic acid - - - 30 grains.
> Alcohol - - - - - 4 drachms.
> Water - - - - - 4 drachms.

Shake the mixture well up, and pour it again upon the plate. The picture will now soon begin to appear, and will proceed until all the detail is well out; but develop as long as you like, the picture remains quite faint of a reddish hue—it is a phantom picture. More of the pyrogallic acid will hasten the development if the picture is quite slow in making its appearance.

The plate is now gently washed and flowed with dilute acetic acid to remove the alkali; and all the intensity you desire may be communicated to it by now treating the film with the acid developer before given, adding more of the silver solution to get great opacity. When the acid developer becomes red or turbid, it is better to prepare a fresh solution, otherwise you might produce stains or asperities, which can not be removed afterward.

CHAPTER XI.

TRANSPARENT positives are prepared upon glass, and are positive pictures seen by transmitted light; they are consequently quite distinct from ambrotypes, which are also positives on glsss, but these, to be seen by reflected light, are, like daguerreotypes, inverted laterally.

A transparent positive may be made either in the camera or by contact printing. We have, consequently, two cases:

POSITIVE PRINTING ON GLASS BY MEANS OF THE CAMERA.

For this sort of printing, a copying camera is an absolute necessity, a *sine qua non*, as the Professor of Latin is always drumming into the ears of his lay brethren.

Now, a copying is compound in form, but yet a very simple apparatus. It consists, essentially, of two cameras, one finished with a lens, and the other not; these two cameras are screwed tightly together, endwise, so that the bellows parts open in opposite directions; one of these is intended to receive the negative, and the other the sensitized glass, which is to receive the actinic impression or the transparent positive. The tablets which hold both the positive and the negative, are furnished with spring clamps, either in the corners or on the sides which are designated to hold the respective glasses in their places.

As we have already remarked in a preceding chapter, the negatives, which are in the best condition for such like work as here comprehended, are very thin, transparent and full of detail; we have described how such negatives have to be prepared. Place such a negative wrong side up in the shield, the collodion film looking toward the lens; from such an arrangement it is evident the copy in the conjugate focus of the camera will be in its true and natural position; that is not inverted. The sensitized is introduced, when ready, into the opposite bellows, with the collodion film facing the lens.   .

The focussing requires more than ordinary care; in fact, you must be furnished with a magnifying lens, which has already been adjusted in focus to the ground glass surface, when it fits in contact with the back of the ground glass plate. The camera may be placed in such a direction as to receive the full light of the sun upon the negative, both during focussing and printing.

With a copying camera it is easy to find the equivalent focus of your compound lens. We mean by this equivalent value, the focal length of a double convex lens that will produce a picture of an object of exactly the same size as that produced by the combination, when the distance from the object to the lens is in either case the same. When two such dissimilar lenses thus produce the same result as to magnitude, we say they are endowed with equivalent foci; but the optical center of a double convex lens is its geometrical center, and consequently is very easily found, the moment we know the thickness; and the distance of this center from the true burning point is denominated the focal distance, this being the focal distance of parallel rays, and is likewise easily measured by a practical experiment. Furthermore, the distance between the object (that is, the negative) and the ground glass, when the pictures on the negative and the ground glass are just of the same size, is four times the length of the focal distance; hence, if we focus the negative so that the picture on the ground glass is accurately of the same, and then measure the distance between the two interior surfaces of the negative and of the ground glass, and divide this distance afterward by four, we obtain the equivalent focus of one compound lens.

Again, if the negative be brought nearer to the lens than twice the focal length of the lens, the ground glass will have to retire from the lens on the opposite side, but not in the same ratio, but with an increasing velocity; and the picture produced by such an arrangement will gradually and quickly increase in size. But if you once know the focal power of the lens and, at the same time, you measure the distance from the negative to the center of the combination, which is an approximation to the optical center, you can, by calculation, tell the distance at which the ground glass has to be placed in order to produce a sharp picture; that is, a picture in focus.

The formula by which the calculation is to be made is as follows:

$$v = \frac{f\,(n+1)}{n}$$

5

in which v represents the required distance of the ground glass, f represents the equivalent focus, n the number of times the picture on the ground glass is to be greater or less than the object or picture on the negative. In plain arithmetic add one to the number of times the picture on the ground glass is to be greater or less than that on the negative; multiply this sum by the equivalent focal length, and finally divide the product by the number of times the picture on the ground glass is greater or less than that on the negative.

The time of exposure in the copying camera will vary with the power of the lens and the magnitude of the picture. A picture of the same size as the original negative, with a one-fourth compound lens, stopped down to a circle of half an inch in diameter, in the direct light of the sun, will require about ten or fifteen seconds' exposure.

The collodion, the silver bath, and all other materials used in developing and fixing are the same in this process as in the ordinary negative process. The mode of development is slightly modified; either the development must not be carried on as far as for a negative, or the developer must be rendered more acid; the object of either of these provisoes is to preserve the picture quite clear in the lights. Carey Lea's ferro-gelatine developer is excellent for this purpose.

Use fresh fixing solution for each plate, and wash very thoroughly. Transparent positives require toning; this is easily effected with the solution of terchloride of gold, and that of acid bichloride of mercury, as previously recommended in the intensifying process as applied to negatives. After which the plate is again carefully washed and varnished with a colorless and transparent varnish prepared as follows:

VARNISH FOR TRANSPARENT POSITIVES.

Copal (tender) - - - -	1 ounce.
Mastic (in tears) - - -	80 grains.
Venice turpentine - - -	50 minims.
Alcohol (95 per cent.) 10 drachms, (fluid measure.)	

Apply the varnish to the cold, but dry plate, and allow it to dry spontaneously.

TO PREPARE TRANSPARENT POSITIVES BY CONTACT PRINTING.

This process requires the use of dry plates, and is certainly one of the most interesting of processes in photography. The tannin plate will suit our purpose very well, but a plate prepared according to one of the modified Fothergill processes will produce a positive better than can be obtained by the tannin process; the most beautiful transparent positive is prepared by what is denominated the albumen process, which is more difficult of manipulation than the preceding. If the dry tannin plate be used, it will be necessary both in the development and in the intensifying operation to acidify the pyrogallic acid with either citric or nitric acid instead of acetic acid, which latter communicates to the picture a reddish tone. The picture may be toned afterward with terchloride of gold and the acid bichloride of mercury in the usual way.

The negative is placed first in the ordinary printing-frame, the film being upward; upon this is laid the prepared dry plate, the collodion film being downward; that is the two films are in contact. The frame

is now closed, laid upon a small, flat board, to keep out
the light, and is then carried out of the dark-room,
where it is turned up and exposed for one or two
seconds to the diffused light of day; or it may be exposed for ten or more seconds to the light issuing from
a gas jet or from a piece of burning phosphorus or
magnesium.   The plateholder is then turned over
again flat upon the small piece of board and carried
back into the dark-room, where it is developed like
any other tannin plate.

TO PREPARE DRY PLATES BY GORDON'S PROCESS.

Any good bromo-iodized collodion is suitable in this
process; and the plate requires no previous substratum
of albumen or other material.   Besides this, the plate
may be sensitized in the ordinary bath of nitrate of
silver, made slightly acid with nitric acid.   All these
are advantages in favor of this process.

After the plate has been properly excited or sensitized in the silver solution, it is placed in a dish or
basin of distilled water, where it remains until a second
plate is so prepared as to take its place, when it is
transferred to a second basin of distilled water.   After
this it is washed gently at the tap and coated with the
preservative solution.

Have prepared the following stock solutions :

No. 1.—Albumen Stock Solution.

White of egg (well beaten)	-	1 ounce.
Distilled water	- - -	4 drachms.
Liq. ammoniæ	- - -	5 minims.

No. 2.—Stock Solution of Nitrate of Silver.

Nitrate of silver	- - -	30 grains.
Distilled water	- - -	1 ounce.

From these solutions you prepare another every time a plate is ready as follows:

Preservative Solution for Present Use.

Of the prepared albumen -   -   4 drachms.
Ammonia   -   -   -   -   5 minims.
Nitrate of silver solution -   -   15   "

This solution is prepared as follows: Measure out in a separate vessel the five minims of ammonia, then add the nitrate of silver solution; this mixture is finally added to the half ounce of albumen, and, after the mixture has been well shaken, the mucilaginous-like material is poured upon the plate so as to cover it, moved backward and forward upon the plate, and then the excess is poured back into the vial. A sufficient quantity will be left with which to coat a second plate; or, instead of this, half the quantity may be prepared at a time for each stereoscopic plate. After the plate has been thus treated, it is carefully and evenly washed with one pint of water made to flow from the narrow orifice of a long spout like that on an oil can; it is finally swilled with distilled water and placed away in a perfect light tight box to dry spontaneously.

Exposure.

The plate is exposed about the same length of time as that required for a tannin plate with the alkaline developer, or about four or five times as long as is required for the wet process.

Development.

Flush the plate with distilled water and afterward with a solution of plain pyrogallic acid. Dissolve, for

instance, ninety-six grains of pyrogallic acid in an
ounce of alcohol, and afterward measure out five minims (not drops) of the solution and mix it with four
drachms of water.

Let the solution flow backward and forward over
the plate for four or five minutes ; at the expiration of this time, or perhaps even before, the image
will be complete in all its detail, although it will be
nothing more than a phantom image. In order to in-
tensify this phantom image, you now pour out again
five minims of the pyrogallic acid solution to half an
ounce of water, to which are added a couple of drops
of the following silver solution :

Acid Nitrate of Silver.

Nitrate of silver - - - -	30 grains.
Citric acid - - - - -	40 "
Distilled water - - - -	1 ounce.

The image now soon begins to show more vigor, and
gradually becomes more intense. Proceed slowly and
patiently until the picture is complete. If there are
any signs of under-exposure, use the smallest quantity
of silver; whereas, when the plate has been over-exposed, a larger quantity of silver becomes quite necessary. With plates prepared by Gordon's method, the
final tone of the negative depends, as is the case in the
tannin process, on the acid allied with the pyrogallic
acid, thus in the present instance, when citro-nitrate
of silver is used, the color of the negative has an olive
tinge, whilst with aceto-nitrate of silver it has a choco-
late reddish hue. It is not necessary to push the intensity to the extent required in a wet plate, because

of the non-actinic color of the negative produced by either the tannin or this modified Fothergill process.

If the operator be desirous of getting a vigorous final tone of a purple black color, he can do it by the application of the toning and intensifying process with terchloride of gold and acid bichloride of mercury.

There is no danger of the film slipping off the plate by this process; and if there is any tendency to blisters, these can be obviated by adding to the fixing solution a small quantity of alcohol. It is preferable to use only a fresh solution of hyposulphite of soda in fixing the dry plate negative.

TO PREPARE TRANSPARENT STEREOGRAPHS.

The chemical parts of this operation are in no way changed from those just given for making any other transparent positive; but, inasmuch as a stereoscopic negative produces prints which are laterally inverted, the right picture being on the left side of the paper, whilst the left picture is on the right side, it becomes necessary to cut the stereoscopic negative in two and mutually to transpose the two halves and to mount them on a separate glass. The proper plan is to cut the two glass pictures down to the required size which the paper prints are to have, and then to mount them with a little transparent cement along the edges to the glass support beneath.

As soon as the stereoscopic negative has thus been transformed, we may place it in the printing-frame and obtain from it by contact printing a copy in which there will be no lateral inversion of the individual prints, and in which the right picture is on the right side and the left picture on the left side.

There is another method of preparing a stereoscopic negative for contact printing; it is a very interesting method, and consists in first obtaining a transparent positive from the negative by means of two stereoscopic lenses placed side by side, and then from this positive to obtain a negative by means of a single orthoscopic lens.

To effect the right conditions, the original negative is placed wrong side up, and with the film facing the lenses, in the copying camera; an impression is then taken on a sensitized plate in the other bellows part of the camera. The copy is a transparent positive, which, when finished, is placed in front of the lenses, the film looking toward the lenses; these lenses are now taken out, and a single orthoscopic or globe lens is substituted in their place. A sensitized plate being placed on the opposite side, a copy is taken which will be a negative endowed with the requisite transformation for contact printing.

But by camera printing a transparent stereoscopic positive is obtained without the trouble of two operations. All that is required is to copy the original negative by means of two lenses as just described, the resulting copy is a transparent stereoscopic positive devoid of lateral inversion of every kind.

By any one of the three methods above described, the picture is on the front of the glass, and on this account it requires two extra glasses when mounted, a thin ground glass behind, and a similarly thin transparent glass in front. By such a method there is, therefore, a loss of material, and our aim naturally is to obtain a picture free from all inversion when seen on the back of the glass and not in front.

To effect this, that is, to prepare a transparent positive on the back of the glass there are several methods, which the ingenious operator can easily find out himself; we will describe only two. Take the original negative, turn it wrong side up, and place it in the shield of the copying camera, the film being outward; copy this negative by means of two lenses, the resulting copy will be a transparent positive on the back of the glass free from transposition, obtained by direct camera printing. A second method consists in first getting a negative so transposed as to allow the requisite prints to be made correctly by contact printing. This negative is obtained as follows:

Let the film of the original negative look outward and take a copy as before by means of two lenses; afterward copy the positive by means of a single lens, the film looking inward toward the lens.

More extensive information on this subject may be obtained by consulting the author's treatise denominated "Dry Plate Photography."

CHAPTER XII.

THIS is an interesting branch of photography, because the resulting pictures are exceedingly beautiful. Opal or porcelain plates are translucent and of a milky color; they may be obtained from the photographic dealers of any size required. Those which are not perfectly flat, are used for camera printing; whilst those which are quite flat originally, or ground flat, are used chiefly for contact printing. Hence, there are two methods by which opal pictures may be prepared: by the wet, and by the dry process.

BY THE WET PROCESS.

Clean the plates like any other or the ordinary glass plates, and then coat them with a dilute solution of albumen, and put them away to dry.

The negative, which is suitable for such like operations, must be taken specially for the purpose with the dilute collodion and by the method already described in reference to copying and solar enlargements. Place the negative inverted in the copying camera, the film facing the lens. A sensitized opal plate is then placed in the opposite bellows of the camera. It is customary to print opal pictures of the vignette shape; this is effected by a vertical frame parallel with the negative and capable of sliding between the lens and the negative. This parallel frame is covered with an opaque plate of thin metal or block cardboard, in the middle of which there is an elliptical opening designed to produce the vignette. Around the edge of the elliptical opening a piece of tissue is gummed, and a smaller elliptical opening is cut through this tissue paper, concentric with the larger. The edge of this tissue paper is then cut with a very sharp knife or a pair of scissors into fine arrow like projections all around. Any variety, shape and size of vignette can thus be prepared and attached to the moving vertical slide; and by moving the slide nearer to the negative or further from it, a given vignette can be diminished or increased in size *ad libitum* within certain limits.

The copying camera is placed so as to receive the direct rays of the sun, or the bright, white light from a cloud in the opposite part of the heavens to the sun; in this position the sensitized plate is exposed for fifteen seconds or more according to the intensity of the light and other circumstances connected with the lenses and negative. The opal plate is then taken into the dark-room where the picture is developed.

The ordinary iron developer is used for this purpose, taking care, however, to make it slightly more acid than for ordinary operations; thus, take half an ounce of the developer, which will be sufficient for a common card-picture, and add to it one drop of nitric acid. Shake the developer and pour it uniformly and quickly over the plate so as to cover it without any line of stoppage. Develop until all detail is out, and then stop immediately. Wash the plate carefully and fix with a fresh solution of either cyanide of potassium, or hyposulphite of soda. Finally, wash again very carefully and thoroughly.

The next part of the operation consists in cleaning off the corners of the plate and removing all stains. This is a delicate manipulation. Prepare tincture of iodine by dissolving a drachm of iodine in one ounce of alcohol. Place before you a wash-basin full of water, and in a convenient place a beaker glass containing solution of cyanide of potassium. Now pour a drop of the tincture of iodine on one of the corners which is stained; it will spread very rapidly and, at the same time, convert the silver stain into soluble iodide of silver; the moment there is any danger of the iodine reaching any part of the picture itself, dip the plate immediately into the water beneath and wash off all the remaining tincture of iodine. Now pour some of the solution of cyanide of potassium upon the same corner where the stain originally existed; the part will become thoroughly bleached; if not, repeat the operation with the tincture and cyanide until the stain is removed. Every other stain is treated in the same manner. If the picture itself is stained, there is no alternative but to make a new picture, because you cannot remove such a stain without, at the same time, bleaching some of the fine markings of the picture itself.

We will suppose the plate has, however, been completely cleaned by the process prescribed; we now proceed a step further and tone our picture. Flow over the plate a dilute solution of terchloride of gold until the tone is uniformly changed all over the plate; then wash the plate. If it is intended to color the picture by stippling or otherwise, it will not be necessary to proceed any further; but where it is intended not to apply any color whatever, the tone of the picture may be considerably improved by flowing over the plate the dilute solution of bichloride of mercury, consisting of fifteen minims of a saturated solution of bichloride of mercury, fifteen minims of acetic acid and four drachms of water. The intensity of the picture will increase very rapidly to a certain extent, and then it retrogrades; you must be careful, therefore, to stop its action in time; in fact the picture seldom requires more than just to be covered with the solution and then carefully washed. After this operation the plate is thoroughly washed and afterward dried. If the plate is to be mounted in a case with a glass in front of it, it will not be necessary to apply any varnish; but if a varnish is to be used, it must be of a very fine nature and nearly colorless.

An opal picture admits of being stippled so as to imitate a perfect miniature gem of art, unsurpassed by any other production of the same nature.

Owing to the innumerable stains which almost invariably are seen in stern contrast with the white porcelain, operators in general prefer preparing these opal pictures by some of the dry processes; and of these dry processes the collodio-chloride process of Dr. G. Wharton Simpson is by far the most expeditious.

COLLODIO-CHLORIDE PROCESS.

In this process the collodion itself is made sensitive, and consequently requires to be kept in a dark cupboard. It is better, also, to surround the bottle, in which it is contained, with some non-actinic material such as a metallic case or with several folds of yellow paper or cloth.

Prepare the following stock solutions:

No. 1.

Nitrate of silver	- - -	ˉ2 drachms.
Distilled water	- - -	2 "

No. 2.

Chloride of calcium	- -	64 grains.
Alcohol -	- - - -	2 ounces.

No. 3.

Citric acid	- - - -	64 grains.
Alcohol -	- - - -	2 ounces.

When about to use this process, prepare the following solution for present use:

Collodio-Chloride.

Plain collodion -   -   -   - 2 ounces.
Nitrate of silver solution, No. 1, 30 minims; Alcohol, 1 drachm, previously mixed.
Chloride of calcium solution, No. 2, 1 drachm.
Citric acid solution, No. 3.   -   1 drachm.

Shake this mixture well up and then set it aside to settle; in a quarter of an hour it will be ready for use. By this arrangement small quantities of the collodio-chloride can be prepared quite easily; it is, therefore, much better to prepare only just sufficient for the occasion.

The albumenized plates are coated with this emulsive collodion as with any other collodion, and then reared up to dry. When they are quite dry, they may be albumenized in the usual way for about five minutes; this part of the operation is, however, not absolutely necessary; it is optional.

After this operation the dry collodio-plate is ready for exposure. Of course the reader must understand that for this process we make use only of *flat* plates, either ground or unground, because in the printing operation they have to lie in close apposition with the negative, which must, also, have been taken on flat plate glass.

There are several printing-frames made specially for this sort of printing; for an ordinary printing-frame will not permit you to examine the printing as it advances. Shive was the first to get up an opal printing-frame, which, with all the accessories that have since been added, is the most complete. Chapman's opal printing-frame, as also Anthony's pneumatic porcelain printing-frame, is exceedingly ingenious and appropriate for the purpose in view.

The negative is placed in the printing-frame first, and upon this comes the sensitized opal plate, the two films, of course, being in contact; by the peculiarity of construction of such printing-frames, the opal plate can be raised from the negative, when occasion requires to examine the progress of printing, and can again be replaced without disturbing the relative position of the negative and the opal plate. The print is precisely like an albumen print; it is produced directly by the light of the sun, and consequently requires no development after it leaves the frame. A slight over-exposure is necessary. When the image is thoroughly brought out and bronzing is just commencing, the opal plate is taken from the frame and washed by immersing it in rain water and by oscillating it so as to remove any free nitrate of silver. It is then transferred to a weak toning bath, where it remains until it is satisfactory. From this bath it is removed to a vessel of clean water where it is again washed, and afterward transferred to the fixing solution of fresh hyposulphite containing a little alcohol, which renders the film more porous and less liable to blister. Finally, wash the plate and dry it. It is now ready for the artist to be stippled or colored as fancy, fashion or taste may suggest.

TO PRINT OPAL PICTURES BY DEVELOPMENT.

The plate is exposed either in the camera or in the printing-frame as usual, but for a very short time, after which the picture is brought out by development. The developer used is that of gallic acid and acetate of lead, as recommended by M. Carey Lea, Esq.

Gallic acid - - - - -	6 grains.
Acetate of lead - - - -	3 "
Rain water - - - - -	40 ounces.

The precipitate of gallate of lead is dissolved by adding a few drops of glacial acetic acid. The opal plate is immersed in this bath until the proper intensity is acquired. It is then washed, toned and fixed as before.

CHAPTER XIII.

THESE prints are positives to be seen by reflected light, and are in reality a sort of incipient negatives; negatives not yet arrived at maturity. In these prints the silver deposit, by reason of its whiteness projected on a black background forms the lights, whilst the shades are produced by the background seen through the film, and, in the case of ambrotypes, through the glass medium on which the picture is made. Fresh and uncontaminated silver solutions and developers are required in the production of pure and rich positives of this nature.

Japanned plates or paper may be had already prepared at the photographic establishments for the preparation of melainotypes, ferrotypes, etc. ; whilst for ambrotypes thin, white or transparent plate glass is used.

FERROTYPE OR MELAINOTYPE.

If the plate has not been used before, brush off the dust with a camel's hair pencil, or polish it with a piece of fine buckskin if necessary, then coat it with rather a thin cadmium collodion and sensitize the plate in the usual manner.

The plate, after draining, is then placed in the printing-frame and a piece of glass plate is placed on the back of it in order that the pressure of the lid or door of the printing-frame may be equal all over. The exposure may be a trifling less than for a negative.

DEVELOPMENT OF A MELAINOTYPE.

None of the organico-iron developers are so well adapted for the production of a rich melainotype, as the ordinary and unsophisticated protosulphate of iron developer.

Developer for Melainotypes.

Protosulphate of iron - -	2 drachms.
Acetic acid - - - -	2 "
Alcohol - - - - -	1 "
Rain water - - - -	8 ounces.

To produce a more metallic and silvery appearance, the following formula has been much recommended:

Protosulphate of iron - -	2 drachms.
Acetic acid - - - -	2 "
Alcohol - - - - -	1 drachm.
Nitrate of potassa - - -	30 grains.
Nitrate of silver solution (30 grs.	
to the ounce) - - -	30 minims.
Nitric acid - - - -	6 "

Pour the developer quickly over the plate, holding the edge of the vial close to the plate, in order that the momentum produced by the fall of the fluid may not produce a white speck on the plate beneath. As soon as the image appears in full detail and before the intensifying process sets in, the plate must be washed. The knack is to find out exactly the right time when to stop the development. It is as we have described it, the moment between the two operations : that of developing the picture, and that of intensifying the picture. The eye soon becomes inured to the change of phenomena. It may happen that the detail does not all appear before the transition from one subdivision to the other takes place; in this case the exposure has been too short; on the other hand, the development is so rapid as not to permit one to catch the exact moment when to stop, and the plate becomes universally veiled by the silver reduction on the lights themselves; in this case the exposure was altogether too long. You have, naturally, to study the capacity of the lens with a given light, and its general working powers ; you can then easily appromixate to the right time of exposure on a given day. The requisites of a good melainotype are perfect transparency of the glass in the deepest shades, complete detail in every part and a general brightness in the picture. If there is any veil or fogging on the transparent parts, that is, those parts which are to form the deep shadows, the picture is a failure, and you will have to take it over again.

Supposing you have hit upon the right exposure, and have developed just far enough, wash the print and then fix it with the ordinary solution of cyanide of potassium, and finally wash and dry the plate.

All that now remains is to color it according to taste and then varnish; or, which is still better, to varnish it first and color it afterward with very fine colors in powder.

It is customary to mount the melainotype in a case, placing a mat first over the print and then a piece of polished plate glass ; these are bound close together with the appropriate preserver, and finally fixed or inserted in the case.

AMBROTYPES.

An ambrotype is a positive on glass. The thinnest white, that is, colorless plate glass, as far as is compatible with strength, is the best for this purpose. The operations in every respect are the same in preparing an ambrotype as those performed in the preparation of a melainotype. When the print or picture is complete, and has been caryfully washed, it is dried. It is now ready for mounting.

It was customary, at an early date, to coat the back of the plate with a thick black Japan, or varnish composed as follows :

BLACK VARNISH.

Asphaltum - - - -	2 ounces.
Canada balsam - - - -	4 "
Oil of turpentine - - -	50 "

This varnish was laid on so as to form a uniform coating and then dried. It is much easier, however, to cut out a piece of black velvet of the size of the plate and place it behind the picture. A mat is placed over the picture, and a plate of glass is placed over the mat; whilst another plate lies behind the velvet to keep it uniformly in apposition with the back of the plate. All these appendages are bound firmly together with the preserver, and then inserted in the appropriate case.

CHAPTER XIV.

THE solar camera is in reality a copying camera, with the simple addition of a lens or other attachment, by means of which the sun light can be condensed upon the negative, and thus made more powerful. There are two distinct kinds of solar cameras; one is fixed in its place, and the sun, by means of a reflector, is made to shine along the axis in whatever part of the heavens this orb may happen to be. The other is suspended on two axes, a vertical and a horizontal, and is thus capable of moving in any direction whatever, and consequently of following the sun's motion, both in altitude and azimuth. All solar cameras of the first class, are *exact* imitations of the well-known solar microscope. Woodward's solar camera was the first in date, and, wonderful enough, it is protected with a patent! although the special function of the solar microscope, previous to this patent grant, was to produce a picture, on a screen behind the lens, of another picture or object placed in the conjugate focus in front. Some improvements, in the way of directing the reflector horizontally and vertically, have since been made in this camera, for instance, in Gale's improved camera; and some have attached to them an arrangement of clockwork, called a Heliostat, which regulates the motion of the reflector according to the motion of the sun, and thus keeps the sun's rays always parallel

with the axis of the instrument.   This attachment
makes this sort of solar camera, in one sense of the
word, perfect.   Such a camera is fixed in a window
facing the South.   This window is boarded up, so that
no light can enter the room, excepting through the
lens.   This room becomes, therefore, the dark chamber,
the camera obscura.   The screen which receives the
image is movable upon the floor behind, so that it can
be brought nearer to the lens or well drawn from it,
according to the size of the picture required.   This is
a convenient property of this sort of camera, an advantage which cameras of the second class do not
possess to the same extent.   The general construction
of Woodward's solar camera and of all its congeners,
is as follows: First comes a rectangular reflector, placed
outside the window, and capable of moving vertically
and horizontally, and of thus reflecting the sun's rays
perpendicularly upon a condensing lens, which is generally a plano-convex lens, the convex surface receiving
the rays.   The negative comes next in order; it is inverted, and the film looks toward the portrait lens, and
is capable of motion to and from this lens by means of
a horizontal slide.   The portrait lens or distributing
lens, comes next; it is fixed upon a frame which slides
horizontally.   The axis of this instrument is a line
which passes through the center of the condensing
lens, of the picture and of the portrait lens, which
latter is placed at such a distance from the condensing
lens as to allow the cone of condensed light to come
to a focus in the optical center of the combination, or
at least in such a position that the conjugate cone of
light, and that of the picture itself, shall occupy as

nearly as possible the same position, and be of the same size on the screen. To produce this result satisfactorily, requires a certain ratio to exist between the power of the condensing lens and that of the distributing lens. This subject has not met with the study which it deserves; and to the want of accurate knowledge, in this respect, may be attributed the general failure of ordinary operators. If the cone of the condensed light, and if the cone of the picture do not coincide, it is impossible to obtain a picture totally free from what is denominated the ghost, which is a circle of greater actinic force in the center than on the periphery of the illuminated disc, unless the former cone be thrown entirely out of the axis. Another cause that tends to produce this ghost, is to be traced to the spherical and chromatic aberration of the condensing lens. In some instruments this condenser is partially corrected by the interposition of a concave, or a concavo-convex lens, just before the light reaches the negative. This second, or correcting lens, converts the converging rays of light into a parallel beam of light, which simply illuminates the negative with a highly condensed and nearly uniform light; and then, of course, the two cases, of which we have just above spoken, must of necessity coincide. By such an arrangement, the best work may be expected. Dr. Van Monckhoven's instruments are arranged somewhat in this manner; and the results are well known, and are recommendations of the cameras. The screen, which corresponds to the ground glass in the ordinary camera, is placed vertically behind the distributing lens, and so accurately that its center coincides with the axis of the instrument, and also that the distances of either edge, laterally or vertically to the center of the lens, are in pair respectively the same.

In the portable camera, of which Shive's, Roettger's and Liebert's cameras are examples, there is no reflector. The instrument itself is tilted by the mechanism peculiar to each instrument, so as to receive the direct rays of the sun. This is an advantage over the preceding instrument; because there is always a considerable loss of light after reflection. Another disadvantage of the Woodward, etc. camera, arises especially in Winter, when the sun's altitude is small, and the angle of incidence and of reflection is very large; the light is thus made very weak by such reflection. In the portable solar camera the screen, which is intended to hold the sensitized sheet, has, but comparatively speaking, a short space to move in; and, consequently, with this instrument it is very difficult to obtain life-size figures, because an instrument that would do such work, must, of necessity, be very unwieldy from its size.

To work with the solar camera, we proceed as follows:

Place the negative in its holder, wrong side up, and a large sheet of white paper on the focussing screen. Turn the reflector or the camera, so as to get the illuminated circle of light on the white paper; move the negative until the picture on the paper is sharp all over; by moving the negative nearer to the lens, after it has once been focussed, the screen will have to be shoved further off from the lens on the opposite side, and the picture becomes thereby enlarged; whereas, if the negative be moved back from the lens, the screen will have to be brought nearer, which will make the picture smaller.

As soon as the picture has been accurately focussed, the light is shut off, and the sensitized sheet is fastened to the screen by tacks or otherwise on the place just occupied by the white focussing paper. All being now ready, the light is again turned on; and the operator must see that the sun's rays are continually kept so as to illuminate the same disc to the end of the operation. By means of an aperture or door at the end of the portable camera, and an obturator which subdues the cone of light, you can from time to time observe the progress of the printing.

There are two modes of solar printing, the one direct and the other by continuation or development. The former is the ordinary process of printing with albumen paper, which is sensitized in the usual manner in a large dish of nitrate of silver. Glass, photographic ware or porcelain dishes for this purpose are the best; but dishes made of thin wood, well dried and varnished with two or three coats of varnish, will answer the purpose quite as well and are far from being as expensive as the former. Similar dishes, too, may be used for toning, fixing and washing the prints afterward.

The time of exposure, naturally, will be quite variable, depending, as it does, on so many fortuitous circumstances; but, on an average, a good print may be obtained in about an hour's exposure to bright sunlight. Print until the shades begin to be slightly bronzed.

Tone and fix as usual.

6

PRINTING BY DEVELOPMENT.

There are several methods of printing by development; the following is the one published by Libois in the *Bulletin Belge:*

Take thin Saxony paper and float it for a minute on the following salting solution:

Chloride of ammonium	- -	4 drachms.
Citric acid	- - - -	4 "
Rain water	- - -	25 ounces.

The citric acid is first dissolved in two and a half ounces of water, and completely neutralized by bicarbonate of soda, five drachms of which are required to neutralize three drachms of the acid. The solution of citrate of soda, thus formed, is added to the solution of the chloride of ammonium. The solution must have a slightly acid reaction, which is attained by the addition of a few drops of citric acid in solution. A small quantity of boiled arrowroot is also mixed with this bath, which is said to improve the final tones.

The paper is then hung up to dry, after which it is sensitized by floating it on the following bath for half a minute:

Nitrate of silver -	- - -	1 ounce.
Water	- - - -	18 ounces.

This bath is acidified with a few drops of a solution of citric acid. The first few drops produce a slight precipitate of citrate of silver, which is immediately dissolved by the succeeding drops. When this is effected, the bath is sufficiently acid.

This paper, when dry, is ready to be tacked to the

focussing-screen. You expose until the print assumes a lilac hue, which will be a few minutes at most. The image in this time will be just visible. The paper is now taken out, and immersed in the following developing bath by Carey Lea:

Gallic acid -	-	-	-	-	6 grains.
Acetate of lead -	-	-	-	3	"
Rain water	-	-	-	-	40 ounces.

To be prepared as follows:

Dissolve a drachm of gallic acid in four drachms of alcohol, and a drachm of acetate of lead in twelve ounces and a half of water. Take a drachm of the alcohol solution and twelve drachms and a half of the solution of acetate; add these to one hundred ounces of water, and then drop in just enough glacial acetic acid to redissolve the slight precipitate of acetate of lead that falls.

A number of prints may be immersed at the same time in this bath. The development requires five or six minutes in the dark-room, and is stopped the moment the prints appear perfect; over-printing is not needed; for the fixing solution seems rather to improve the detail than to destroy it.

Wash the prints and then immerse them in the following fixing solution:

Water	-	-	-	-	20 ounces.
Hyposulphite of soda		-	-	6	"

In this bath the prints remain about four minutes, they are then washed thoroughly in a running stream of water. The color of the prints, when they leave the water, is reddish, but it assumes a beautiful deep brown on drying.

Naturally the print may be toned like any other silver print. In this case the print after development is first carefully washed and then immersed in the ordinary gold toning solution, and afterward treated in other respects like any other silver print.

CHAPTER XV.

PICTURES formerly were sometimes surrounded with a border or a garland of twisted vines, whence was derived the name vignette or *little vine*. At present are comprehended under this appellation all pictures of an oval or circular form, situated in the center of the mount, and shading gradually off by a stellar-like gradation into blank space. Card-pictures are most generally so printed; in some instances the pictures are printed as usual in the oval form, but the space which surrounds them is shaded. It is our intention in this chapter to describe this mode of printing.

In the first place the negative itself may be formed into an appropriate condition for printing vignette fashion; but in this case you have to be very careful in focussing to place the sitter always and accurately in the oval of the ground glass which he is to occupy in the print; then, after exposure, the plateholder is taken into the dark-room, and an oval piece of thick leather, with bevelled edges, is placed on the back of the negative in a position to correspond with the given oval of the ground glass. India-rubber ovals might be made on purpose, the under side being formed slightly hollow; these, when pressed down into contact with the glass beneath, will remain, by reason that their elasticity forms a vacuum beneath, firmly adherent to the glass. A piece of tissue paper, somewhat larger than the

India-rubber oval, and cut with star-like indentations on the edge all around, may be gummed upon the back of the India-rubber oval. The plateholder is now taken again into the light, the door or flap is opened, and the plate is exposed for a few seconds to the direct action of the light. It is evident that the part beneath the India-rubber or leather will be protected from the action of light; the tissue paper, projecting beyond the edges, with its stellar projections, softens the abruptness of separation between the picture and the surrounding space. Naturally, the part protected from the light can be made to assume any shape whatever according to the contour of the India-rubber discs. The plateholder is now carried back to the dark-room and the picture is developed. All the parts external to the oval obturator become quite opaque by the development, more opaque than any other part because of the direct exposure to the diffused light; and, consequently, in the print the paper will be preserved quite white, as it ought to be. With a little practice this mode of vignetting is very satisfactory; and the negatives being complete in themselves, you have no further trouble afterward in the printing operation.

Why is it not more generally practiced?

Because, previous to the publication of this treatise, it was not known generally, if at all.

The method in common practice is as follows:

A piece of tin plate, furnished with a rectangular opening in the center larger than the oval vignette, is placed first in the plateholder, then the negative and after that the sensitized paper. Over the rectangular opening there is another tin frame with an oval open-

ing which slides, or is so adjustable so as to bring this
oval opening right over the portrait. A rim of tin is
soldered all around the oval opening about half an
inch or more high, tapering off and forming the frustum of an oval cone as it were. The inside is lined
with black paper, and the aperture is covered over
with tissue paper. Along the edge all around there is
a concentric stellated ring of thicker paper, the star-
like projections of which point to the center of the
oval; another and similar ring, narrower than the
former, is glued upon this upon the outer edge; and
again a third still more narrower than the second. In
this way the light will be impeded into its transition
through the three layers of paper gradually more and
more to the edge of the walls of the frustum; and the
conical shape of this attachment furthermore assists in
softening the gradation of shade into light. The general principle being once known, the operator, if he is
worthy of his profession, can easily modify the different forms of vignetting to his taste and fancy.

Wooden vignettes are easily cut out of a piece of
soft wood, half an inch or more thick, taking care always to bevel the edge gradually toward the negative,
thus making the opening nearest the negative larger
than that on which the tissue paper is glued or
gummed.

When printing with a vignette of this construction
it is necessary to print with diffused light, if the plateholder is to remain quiescent when once laid down;
but if the light is direct solar light, or a very bright reflected light from an illuminated cloud or surface, the
plateholder must be gradually turned around in order

to equallize the illumination and thus soften the shadows.

Another mode of vignetting consists in placing, first in the plateholder, a so-called glass vignette. This glass vignette is of the same size as the plate you are using; that is, you may procure a quarter-plate vignette, a half-plate, or a whole, etc., plate vignette. These plates are made of glass stained of an orange-red or yellow color, and are non-actinic; but the central part of the stain, which is superficial, is ground off on either side of the plate of an oval shape, and the plain glass beneath is then polished. These vignette glasses are very convenient and highly satisfactory if the color happens to be of the right nature. Two or three of these glasses with various sized openings may be placed one over the other, the smallest opening being outermost or most remote from the negative.

TO PRINT A DARK BORDER.

In order to print a dark border around a light oval vignette, you take the print out from the printing-frame when the picture is sufficiently advanced to be called finished, and place an oval obturator of the proper size over the portrait and a portion of the white surrounding paper. The paper is then exposed to diffused light until the tone is suitable. It is well to turn the platform which holds the paper gradually around during this exposure, otherwise the shade will not be uniform.

Landscapes may be printed of the desired shape by placing the proper shaped mat in front of the negative.

When printing either with the copying camera, or

the solar camera, it is immaterial in principle whether the vignette is placed between the negative and the lens, or between the print and the lens; it is sometimes more mechanically advantageous the one way than it is the other.

The toning, fixing and washing of a vignetted print require no instruction; they naturally are the same with this as any other print.

CHAPTER XVI.

THE MAGIC PRINT.

THE magic print is one that is developed by the superimposition of a piece of moist paper upon a piece of albumen paper which apparently contains no picture. The operation looks like a feat of the enchanter.

The magic papers, the invisible prints, are prepared as follows:

Print on albumen paper from the negative in the usual way, but take the prints out whilst they are still somewhat weak, but still complete in detail; that is, you must not over print for this purpose.

The prints are then taken out, washed and fixed in hyposulphite of soda, again *thoroughly* washed, and then submitted to a bleaching process.

The bleaching, properly whitening solution, consists of bichloride of mercury:

Bichloride of mercury	- -	1 drachm.
Water - - - -	-	4 ounces.

Immerse the moist prints in this solution and keep them there until the pictures disappear. They are now again thoroughly washed, dried and packed away between folds of clean paper.

These magic papers are developed in the following manner:

Dip pieces of blotting paper in a solution of hypo-sulphite of soda, and whilst still moist place one over each albumen magic paper and put a weight over it to keep it in close apposition. The print will gradually reappear. When completely redeveloped the print is thoroughly washed and dried. It will now keep for an indefinite time.

The solution of bichloride of mercury does not destroy the image, but simply combines with its silver and forms a double salt which is white. This experiment is quite analogous to that when oxalic acid in solution is placed upon writing with common iron ink; the writing disappears, but it still remains in the paper, it has simply become white writing, instead of black.

We have in the preceding chapters recommended the use of bichloride of mercury as an intensifier, but the reader must be careful not to carry the intensification so far as finally to whiten the print. At the beginning of the redevelopment the image grows more and more black, then it gradually from this point becomes more and more white (not transparent). The operator can easily see when to stop.

CHAPTER XVII.

WHAT TO DO WITH THE SILVER AND GOLD RESIDUES.

THE nitrate of silver in all the old residues of the sensitizing baths both for paper and for plates, is reduced to the state of chloride of silver by the addition of a solution.

The chloride is a white powder and soon settles to the bottom of the vessel; the supernatant liquid is then poured into another vessel, and again solution of salt is added to it; if no further precipitate of chloride of silver is produced, this liquid is thrown away. On the contrary, if any chloride is still produced, add solution of salt until the reduction is complete; decant as before, and add the residue to the other. Wash the white precipitate in several changes of water, allowing the silver salt to settle each time and then decanting the clear portions.

This white chloride of silver may easily be reduced to pure silver without the aid of fire. Keep the salt under water in the dark-room until you have enough to operate upon, and time to devote to the operation. The following is the mode of reduction:

Take a bar of clean zinc as heavy as the quantity of chloride to be reduced, and solder to one end of it a silver wire; then cover the zinc completely with fine gauze or muslin and dip it in clean water. Now immerse the zinc, so covered, in the moist chloride of silver, and bend over the other end of the silver wire

so as to come in contact with the chloride of silver at
a short distance from the remote end of the zinc. The
operation is best conducted in the dark-room. The
moment the connection is made with the silver wire
and the chloride, an electric current sets in and decomposes the chloride of silver into pure silver, which
manifests itself first at the loose end of the silver wire.
The chlorine which is set free hastens through the
muslin and combines with the zinc, forming chloride
of zinc, a very soluble salt which remains in solution.
The operation may continue until all the white chloride
has changed color and become silver gray. The bar
of zinc is now taken out and washed to remove any adhering silver; it is much lighter than it was before the
operation. Dilute sulphuric acid is added to the silver
powder in order to dissolve any particles of zinc; after
settling a number of hours the supernatant liquid is
poured away, and the residue is well washed in several
changes of water. This residue is pure silver containing still, probably, some undecomposed chloride of
silver, which is no injury to it. The residue is finally
mixed with nitric acid containing an equal volume.of
water; it is soon dissolved. If any chloride was in the
silver powder, it will be found now at the bottom of
the vessel undissolved, and can easily be separated by
decantation. This solution is then evaporated to dryness on a water bath, and the residue is again dissolved in a small quantity of hot water and put aside
to crystallize. The mother liquor, or that part which
cannot be made to crystallize, may be used for the sensitizing bath for paper, after it has once more evaporated to dryness.

The undissolved portion of chloride of silver, if any there were, may be added to the next batch and treated with it as before directed.

TO REDUCE THE CHLORIDE AND OXIDE OF SILVER BY FIRE.

The method we have just described is a very reliable one; but still, if you have the convenience, you may reduce the residues to pure silver by fire; and the advantage here is that different residues, as for instance, the chloride and the oxide, etc., may be mixed together and reduced at the same time. The paper scraps, as we have already told you, are burnt in a clean stove; by this act the silver compound is reduced to a mixture of silver and oxide of silver which will form the ashes. These ashes and the chloride obtained from the old baths, and the powder from the developing solutions, are all first thoroughly dried and then intimately mixed with twice their weight of carbonate of soda and chalk. The mixture is put into a crucible which is heated afterward in a furnace to a very high temperature, at which it is maintained until the silver salts are thoroughly reduced. The mass is kept well stirred up with an iron rod from time to time, and at the end the temperature is raised to a white heat and then the crucible is allowed to cool gradually. The silver will be found at the bottom of the vessel; or, whilst the crucible is still at its highest temperature, it is taken out of the fire, and its contents are emptied upon a plate or dish of iron. The silver may be separated from the slag afterward by means of a hammer and a pair of pincers. You will most likely find, also, a number of silver pellets in the mass, which you can pick out with a pair of pliers. The silver is next carefully washed in hot water, and finally dissolved in nitric acid as before in order to make nitrate of silver.

TO REDUCE THE GOLD RESIDUES.

Gold is obtained from old toning baths. The method has already been described of precipitating the gold by means of the protosulphate of iron, and its separation from the silver by means of nitric acid. The gold powder thus obtained may be melted in a clean crucible into a lump of gold at a high temperature. But this would be altogether a loss of labor unless you want to get the value of the gold. As long as you wish merely to convert the gold powder into chloride, the powder is just as good, even better, than gold in the lump, because it is more easily dissolved in the mixed acids in this form.

CHAPTER XVIII.

NEGATIVES of landscapes are best taken in the Spring or Fall of the year; in the Summer season, during the extreme heat, the atmosphere is filled with vapor, which obscures the view with haze; whilst in Winter nature has thrown off her robes of beauty and exhibits herself in a state of dormancy. Still photographs can be taken both in Summer and Winter; and Winter scenery of icebergs and waterfalls is sometimes very grand.

There are two processes for the field, the Wet and the Dry Process. Practical operators will at all times prefer the process with which they are daily familiar; and we would advise them by all means to keep to this process; they will only lose their time and their patience if they meddle with dry plates, however much we may personally approve of them ourselves. We have seen already sufficient of the practice of dry plate photography in the hands of ordinary operators, to sympathize with their failures and to condemn the practice. But whilst we thus warn practical photographers against dabbling in tannin, collodio-albumen and collodio-bromide, we recommend these forbidden practices to the amateur, who can bestow all his energies upon them and is not fettered with the fixed habits of room-work and the wet process.

The great trouble in landscape photography is the weight of materials to be carried into the field, and the construction of a portable dark tent. All the paraphernalia required in the field for the wet process may now, however, be packed into a small compass and are easily transported on a pair of light wheels. We have tried all sorts of tents, and possess four or five kinds. Our tent for stereoscopic purposes is only two feet long, one foot wide and one foot high; and we can operate in it as easily and reliably as in our large laboratory, performing all the operations on the plate until it is ready for varnishing.

Our tent for taking views, ten by twelve inches in size, is at the same time a camera. It folds together into a small compass, and can be mounted in five minutes when once on the ground.

We have also a Carbutt box and tent for field-photography, which we should like exceedingly, if we were not wedded to our own constructions which, to us, appear to work with more satisfaction.

With tents like these it becomes a real pleasure to work in glens, among mountains and waterfalls; and we believe that most of the photographic gems that we receive from Europe, and those of Carbutt, Watkins and others, the Heliographic pioneers of our own country, have been produced by the wet process; and it is well known that very few pictures, taken by the dry process, were to be seen among the artistic photographic productions at the great exhibitions in Europe.

All these facts seem to prove that practical photographers are one-sided in their views, and thus give preference to the wet process; this will no doubt remain so, until—until dry plates are not only as reliable as wet plates, but as easily prepared by the ordinary operator, and with the same collodion and silver bath.

HERMAN ROETTGER, No. 402 Library Street, Philadelphia, Pa.,

Manufacturer of

CAMERAS, SOLAR CAMERAS, LENSES, TELESCOPES, &C.

Price-List of Cameras.

Mammoth Size,	(Centre Stops)	Lenses	6⅛ by 6¼	in. diameter	$350
Extra Double Whole	"	"	5⅛ by 5¼	"	200
Double Whole	"	"	4⅛ by 4¼	"	160
Extra Whole	"	"	3½ by 3⅝	"	120
Whole	"	"	3⅛ by 3¼	"	90
Half	"	"	2⅛ by 2¼	"	45
Quarter	"	"	1½ by 1¾	"	30
Orthoscopic Tube		"	2⅛ by 1½	"	45
" "		"	3 by 2¼	"	70
Twin Tubes, with Centre Stops, for Cartes de Visite					90
Triplets (an improved instrument for landscapes, copying, &c.)					$30 to 100
Solar Camera Tube					45

Roettger's Patent Parallactic Solar Camera.

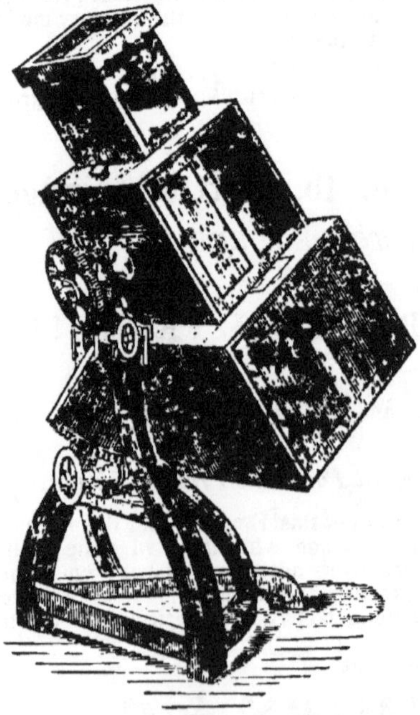

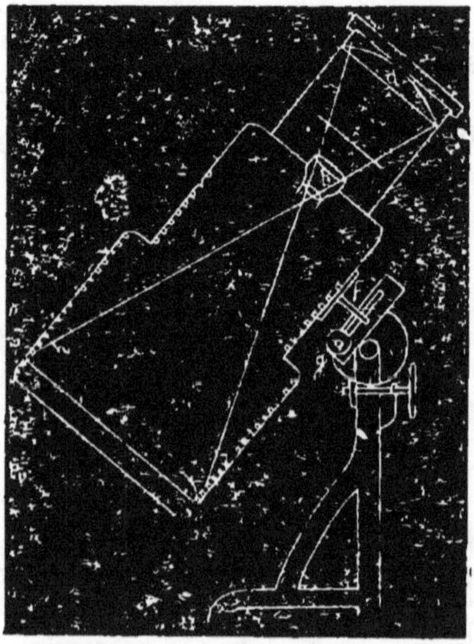

NEW AND IMPORTANT IMPROVEMENT.

We have just patented a great improvement in the Parallactic movement of our Solar Camera, so that it will now follow the course of the sun with unerring certainty. Our Instruments, with this improvement, will soon be in the market.

WAIT AND SEE IT BEFORE PURCHASING.

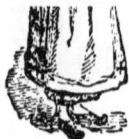

EAGLE PRINTING BOARD!

(PATENTED.)

Fig. 1.   *Fig. 2.*   *Fig. 3.*

The above valuable invention is now ready for sale. Its advantages over the old printing frames, are :

1. It weighs only *one-quarter* as much as the old-fashioned printing frames.
2. It will never break a negative.
3. It can be handled in half the time of any other.
4. It occupies only one-quarter the bulk of any other, and thus saves expense in packing and freight.
5. Twenty-five per cent. more printing can be done with it than with any other, because it can be so much more expeditiously handled.

THE CUTS.

Fig. 1 shows the back of the boards with the brass springs, and a hook or clamp on the end of each, to hold the negative to the board.

Fig. 2 shows the front view, with a negative as it appears when being printed.

Fig. 3 shows the board partly open, to allow the operator to inspect the print, and see how it is progressing.

TESTIMONIALS.

Prof. Towler says : " It is decidedly a neat invention ; so light and yet so strong ; so easy of manipulation, and yet so very appropriate in all its parts. I shall use it altogether in my laboratory."

The Editor of *The Philadelphia Photographer* says : " I think it is very neat indeed, and will be sure to be approved of by all Photographers ; send me half a dozen of each size."

William Campbell says : " It is all I could desire ; so light and so easy of manipulation, and withal so simple, that it must eventually be the only style of Printing Frame used. I recommend it to all."

Oscar G. Mason says : " They are a capital contrivance, and will be sure to have a great sale. It is astonishing that such a frame was never thought of before."

N. G. Burgess says : " It is the neatest thing I have ever seen ; so simple, and yet it answers every purpose better than any other frame in the market. I shall use them altogether in my new gallery."

Augustus Marshall, of Boston, says : " I think the new board is *tip'op;* I only wish I could afford to throw away all my old ones, and get a supply of the Eagles."

And numerous others, which would fill a book to publish.

The following are the

PRICES :

¼ size, each	50 cents.	7 x 9, size, each	$	90
½ "	55 "	8 x 10 "		95
4¼ x 6½ "	60 "	10 x 12 "	1	10
4 x 8 "	70 "	12 x 16 "	2	00
4-4 "	85 "	*Larger sizes made to Order.*		

For Sale by all Stock Dealers.

SARONY'S

PATENT

UNIVERSAL REST

AND

POSING APPARATUS.

Price, Complete with Chair, $100.

NEW INVENTION, BY SARONY, OF SCARBOROUGH, ENGLAND.

———•◦•———

The Apparatus is not easily described in a few words; its use, however, is so simple, that it can be operated by any one who has the skill to make a photograph.

To be fully appreciated it must be seen. It is now in general use in England, France, and Germany. In America it has been adopted by all those who have had the fortune to see it. Among those who have ordered the Apparatus it is only necessary to mention the names of such establishments as Fredricks & Co., Gurney & Son, Brady, Bogardus, Notman and others to secure for it a favorable attention throughout the country.

The following are a few of the opinions of gentlemen who are practically acquainted with the use of the Apparatus:

[From Mr. Notman, Montreal.]

Your patent rest I consider a great boon to photographers, overcoming many long felt difficulties ; and while it gives the photographer more power, it gives to the sitter greater ease and consequently the pictures are more pleasing and graceful.

[From Bogardus' Gallery.]

For easy freedom, artistic effect, and studied ease, combined with perfect solidity of the figure, there is nothing to equal this "Posing Machine" of Mr. Sarony's, which I cheerfully recommend to the Artistic Photographer.

Mr. Sarony is now ready to receive applications for his Posing Apparatus by mail or otherwise, at his rooms No. 543 Broadway, New York. The rest can be had stationary or on a movable platform with castors. Liberal terms granted to Stock Dealers.